15 days
of prayer with
DIETRICH BONHOEFFER

15 days
of prayer/series

On a journey, it's good to have a guide. Even great saints took spiritual directors or confessors with them on their itineraries toward sanctity. Now you can be guided by the most influential spiritual figures of all time. The 15 Days of Prayer series introduces their deepest and most personal thoughts.

This popular series is perfect if you are looking for a gift, or if you want to be introduced to a particular guide and his or her spirituality. Each volume contains:

- ෫ A brief biography of the saint or spiritual leader
- ෫ A guide to creating a format for prayer or retreat
- ෫ Fifteen meditation sessions with focus points and reflection guides

15 days

of prayer with

DIETRICH BONHOEFFER

MATTHIEU ARNOLD

TRANSLATED BY
JACK McDONALD

NEW CITY PRESS
Hyde Park, NY

Published in the United States by New City Press
202 Cardinal Rd., Hyde Park, NY 12538
www.newcitypress.com
©2009 New City Press (English translation)

This book is a translation of *Prier 15 Jours Avec Dietrich Bonhoeffer*, published
by Nouvelle Cité, 2006, Montrouge, France.

Cover design by Durva Correia

Library of Congress Cataloging-in-Publication Data:

A copy of the CIP data is available from the Library of Congress.

ISBN 978-1-56548-311-8

Printed in the United States of America

Contents

How to Use
This Book

*A*n old Chinese proverb, or at least what I am able to recall of what is supposed to be an old Chinese proverb, goes something like this: "Even a journey of a thousand miles begins with a single step." When you think about it, the truth of the proverb is obvious. It is impossible to begin any project, let alone a journey, without taking the first step. I think it might also be true, although I cannot recall if another Chinese proverb says it, "that the first step is often the hardest." Or, as someone else once observed, "the distance between a thought and the corresponding action needed to implement the idea takes the most energy." I don't know who shared that perception with me but I am certain it was not an old Chinese master!

With this ancient proverbial wisdom, and the not-so-ancient wisdom of an unknown contemporary sage still fresh, we move from proverbs to presumptions. How do these relate to the task before us?

I am presuming that if you are reading this introduction it is because you are contemplating a journey. My presumption is that you are preparing for a spiritual journey and that you have taken at least some of the first steps necessary to prepare for this journey. I also presume, and please excuse me if I am making too many presumptions, that in your preparation for the spiritual journey you have determined that you need a guide. From deep within the recesses of your deepest self, there was something that called you to consider Dietrich Bonhoeffer as a potential companion. If my presumptions are correct, may I congratulate you on this decision? I think you have made a wise choice, a choice that can be confirmed by yet another source of wisdom, the wisdom that comes from practical experience.

Even an informal poll of experienced travelers will reveal a common opinion: it is very difficult to travel alone. Some might observe that it is even foolish. Still others may be even stronger in their opinion and go so far as to insist that it is necessary to have a guide, especially when you are traveling into uncharted waters and into territory that you have not yet experienced. I am of the personal opinion that a traveling companion is welcome under all circumstances. The thought of traveling alone, to some exciting destination without someone to share the journey with does not capture my imagination or channel my enthusiasm. However, with that being noted, what is simply a matter of preference on the normal journey becomes a matter of necessity when a person embarks on a spiritual journey.

The spiritual journey, which can be the most challenging of all journeys, is experienced best with a guide, a companion, or at the very least, a friend in whom you have placed your trust. This observation is not a preference or an opinion but rather an established spiritual necessity. All of the great saints with whom I am familiar had a spiritual director or a confessor who journeyed with them. Admittedly, at times the saints might well have traveled far beyond the experience of their guide and companion but more often than not they would return to their director and reflect on their experience. Understood in this sense, the director and companion provided a valuable contribution and necessary resource. When I was learning how to pray (a necessity for anyone who desires to be a full-time and public "religious person"), the community of men that I belong to gave me a great gift. Between my second and third year in college, I was given a one-year sabbatical, with all expenses paid and all of my personal needs met. This period of time was called novitiate. I was officially designated as a novice, a beginner in the spiritual journey, and I was assigned a "master," a person who was willing to lead me. In addition to the master, I was provided with every imaginable book and any other resource that I could possibly need. Even with all that I was provided, I did not learn how to pray because of the books and the unlimited resources, rather it was the master, the companion who was the key to the experience.

One day, after about three months of reading, of quiet and solitude, and of practicing all of the methods and descriptions of prayer that were available to me, the master called. "Put away the books, forget the method, and just listen." We went into a room, became quiet, and tried to recall the presence of God, and then, the master simply prayed out loud and permitted me to listen to his prayer. As he prayed, he revealed his hopes, his dreams, his struggles, his successes, and most of all, his relationship with God. I discovered as I listened that his prayer was deeply intimate but most of all it was self-revealing. As I learned about him, I was led through his life experience to the place where God dwells. At that moment I was able to understand a little bit about what I was supposed to do if I really wanted to pray.

The dynamic of what happened when the master called, invited me to listen, and then revealed his innermost self to me as he communicated with God in prayer, was important. It wasn't so much that the master was trying to reveal to me what needed to be said; he was not inviting me to pray with the same words that he used, but rather that he was trying to bring me to that place within myself where prayer becomes possible. That place, a place of intimacy and of self-awareness, was a necessary stop on the journey and it was a place that I needed to be led to. I could not have easily discovered it on my own.

The purpose of the volume that you hold in your hand is to lead you, over a period of fifteen days or, maybe more realistically, fifteen prayer periods, to a place where prayer is possible. If you already have a regular experience and practice of prayer, perhaps this volume can help lead you to a deeper place, a more intimate relationship with the Lord.

It is important to note that the purpose of this book is not to lead you to a better relationship with Dietrich Bonhoeffer, your spiritual companion. Although your companion will invite you to share some of his deepest and most intimate thoughts, your companion is doing so only to bring you to that place where God dwells. After all, the true measurement of all companions for the journey is that they bring you to the place where you need to be, and then they step back, out of the picture. A guide who brings you to the desired destination and then sticks around is a very unwelcome guest!

Many times I have found myself attracted to a particular idea or method for accomplishing a task, only to discover that what seemed to be inviting and helpful possessed too many details. All of my energy went to the mastery of the details and I soon lost my enthusiasm. In each instance, the book that seemed so promising ended up on my bookshelf, gathering dust. I can assure you, it is not our intention that this book end up in your bookcase, filled with promise, but unable to deliver.

There are three simple rules that need to be followed in order to use this book with a measure of satisfaction.

Place: It is important that you choose a place for reading that provides the necessary atmosphere for reflection and that does not allow for too many distractions. Whatever place you choose needs to be comfortable, have the necessary lighting, and, finally, have a sense of "welcoming" about it. You need to be able to look forward to the experience of the journey. Don't travel steerage if you know you will be more comfortable in first class and if the choice is realistic for you. On the other hand, if first class is a distraction and you feel more comfortable and more yourself in steerage, then it is in steerage that you belong.

My favorite place is an overstuffed and comfortable chair in my bedroom. There is a light over my shoulder, and the chair reclines if I feel a need to recline. Once in a while, I get lucky and the sun comes through my window and bathes the entire room in light. I have other options and other places that are available to me but this is the place that I prefer.

Time: Choose a time during the day when you are most alert and when you are most receptive to reflection, meditation, and prayer. The time that you choose is an essential component. If you are a morning person, for example, you should choose a time that is in the morning. If you are more alert in the afternoon, choose an afternoon time slot; and if evening is your preference, then by all means choose the evening. Try to avoid "peak" periods in your daily routine when you know that you might be disturbed. The time that you choose needs to be your time and needs to work for you.

It is also important that you choose how much time you will spend with your companion each day. For some it will be possible to set aside enough time in order to read and reflect on all the material that is offered for a given day. For others, it might not be possible to devote one time to the suggested material for the day, so the prayer period may need to be extended for two, three, or even more sessions. It is not important how long it takes you; it is only important that it works for you and that you remain committed to that which is possible.

For myself I have found that fifteen minutes in the early morning, while I am still in my robe and pajamas and before my morning coffee, and even before I prepare myself for the day, is the best time. No one expects to see me or to interact with me because I have not yet "announced" the fact that I am awake or even on the move. However, once someone hears me in the bathroom, then my window of opportunity is gone. It is therefore important to me that I use the time that I have identified when it is available to me.

Freedom: It may seem strange to suggest that freedom is the third necessary ingredient, but I have discovered that it is most important. By freedom I understand a certain "stance toward life," a "permission to be myself and to be gentle and understanding of who I am." I am constantly amazed at how the human person so easily sets himself or herself up for disappointment and perceived failure. We so easily make judgments about ourselves and our actions and our choices, and very often those judgments are negative, and not at all helpful.

For instance, what does it really matter if I have chosen a place and a time, and I have missed both the place and the time for three days in a row? What does it matter if I have chosen, in that twilight time before I am completely awake and still a little sleepy, to roll over and to sleep for fifteen minutes more? Does it mean that I am not serious about the journey, that I really don't want to pray, that I am just fooling myself when I say that my prayer time is important to me? Perhaps, but I prefer to believe that it simply means that I am tired and I just wanted a little more sleep. It doesn't mean anything more than that. However, if I make it mean more than that, then I can become discouraged, frustrated, and put myself into a state where I might more easily give up. "What's the use? I might as well forget all about it."

The same sense of freedom applies to the reading and the praying of this text. If I do not find the introduction to each day helpful, I don't need to read it. If I find the questions for reflection at the end of the appointed day repetitive, then I should choose to close the book and go my own way. Even if I discover that the reflection offered for the day is not the one that I prefer and that the one for the next day seems more inviting, then by all means, go on to the one for the next day.

That's it! If you apply these simple rules to your journey you should receive the maximum benefit and you will soon find yourself at your destination. But be prepared to be surprised. If you have never been on a spiritual journey you should know that the "travel brochures" and the other descriptions that you might have heard are nothing compared to the real thing. There is so much more than you can imagine.

A final prayer of blessing suggests itself:

Lord, catch me off guard today.
Surprise me with some moment of
        beauty or pain
So that at least for the moment
I may be startled into seeing that you
        are here in all your splendor,
Always and everywhere,
Barely hidden,
Beneath,
Beyond,
Within this life I breathe.

Frederick Buechner

Rev. Thomas M. Santa, CSsR
Liguori, Missouri

A Brief Chronology of Dietrich Bonhoeffer's Life

4 February 1906:

Birth in Breslau, Germany

1912:

Bonhoeffer's family moves to Berlin

1923-1927:

Bonhoeffer studies theology in Tübingen, Rome and Berlin, finishing with a doctorate entitled *Sanctorum Communio*

1928:

Chaplain of the German Protestant parish in Barcelona

1929-1930:

Teaching Assistant in the University of Berlin

1930-1931:

Extended visit to the USA, including study at Union Theological Seminary

1931:

Privat-Dozent (Assistant Lecturer) at the University of Berlin

30 January 1933:

Adolf Hitler elected Chancellor of the German Reich

24 March 1933:

The German Parliament gives full powers to Hitler

1 February 1933:

Bonhoeffer criticizes Hitler and the "cult of the leader" on German radio

1933-1935:

Extended visit to England

29-31 May 1934:

Free Synod of Barmen breaks with German Protestant Church to found Confessing Church of Protestants hostile to Hitler

Spring 1935:

Bonhoeffer returns to Germany to lead the Confessing Church's seminary at Finkenwalde

August 1936:

Bonhoeffer is forbidden to teach by the German State

1937:

Publishes *On Community Life*

1939:

Publishes *The Price of Grace*

1940:

Enters the German Abwehr (the Counter-Espionage service) but uses his contacts to undermine Hitler by passing information among a group of generals aiming to assassinate him

13 January 1943:

Engaged to marry Maria von Wedermeyer

5 April 1943:

Arrested and imprisoned in Tegel Military Prison, Berlin

20 July 1944:

Failed attempt to assassinate Hitler, led by Hans von Stauffenberg

8 October 1944:

Bonhoeffer transferred to the Gestapo Prison in Berlin

9 April 1945:

Bonhoeffer hanged in Flossenbürg Concentration Camp

A Few Notes on
Dietrich Bonhoeffer

D ietrich Bonhoeffer was born in Breslau, Germany (modern Wroclaw, in Poland) on 4 February 1906. His father, Karl Bonhoeffer, was a university professor of psychiatry and neurology, and his mother, Paula von Hase, was of an aristocratic family. Dietrich and Sabine (his twin sister) were the sixth and seventh of eight children. Later, thanks to Sabine's husband, Gerhard Leibholz, of Jewish origin, Dietrich learned of the fate awaiting German Jews, and began to act to help them.

In 1912, the Bonhoeffers moved to Berlin. From 1923 to 1927, Dietrich read theology at Tübingen, Rome and Berlin. His doctoral thesis, *Sanctorum communio*, expounded a sociological analysis and a theological assessment of the church. In 1928, he spent a year working as an assistant in the German parish in Barcelona. He busied himself there with youth work — and the success he achieved in this area remained with him: to his death, Bonhoeffer was deeply concerned with his students and young colleagues. After a year spent from 1929 to 1930 as an assistant lecturer in the University of Berlin, he completed his education by study-ing from 1930 to 1931 at Union Theological Seminary in New York. This second major time abroad helped Bonhoeffer to develop a great openness of spirit — previously he had nursed a certain bitterness towards France because of the harshness of the terms of the Treaty of Versailles. But thanks to his meetings with the French pacifist Jean Lasserre, he overcame his rancor and steadfastly affirmed the unity of all Christian people against nationalism and the hatred of races or classes.

From 1931, Bonhoeffer taught in the Department of Theology of the University of Berlin, as an associate lecturer (*Privat-Dozent*). At the same time, he was chaplain of the Technische Hochschule in Berlin. During this period he grew to know Karl Barth, then Professor of Theology at the University of Bonn — before Hitler expelled Barth for his opposition to the Nazi régime. On 30 January 1933, Marshal Hindenburg invited Hitler to assume the duties of Chancellor of the German Reich, and on 24 March of the same year, the German parlia-ment gave Hitler full executive powers. From 1

February 1933, Bonhoeffer began to denounce the cult of Hitler. In June, he published an article on "The Church and the Jewish Question." In the same month, the "German-Christians" (Deutsche Christen) — German Protestants who favored collaboration between the Church and Hitler's racist tyranny — became a majority in the Federation of German Protestant Churches.

In October 1933, Bonhoeffer left Germany for England, where until 1935 he was pastor to the German parishes in London. He did not take part in the Free Synod of Barmen (29–31 May 1934), which set up in opposition to the Church of the Reich a Church founded on the Bible and its confessions of faith (from where its name "the Confessing Church" came). The declaration of faith issued by this Synod declared that "the unshakeable foundation of the German Protestant Church is the Gospel of Jesus Christ," and it rejected "the false doctrine that the Church can ... make its message and institutions subject to philosophical or political notions currently in vogue." Although absent from the Synod, Bonhoeffer followed the development of the political and ecclesiastical situation in Germany with care.

When, on 5 September 1933, the Synod of the Old Prussian Church embraced the Aryan Clause of 7 April 1933, which excluded "non-Aryans" from all public offices, Bonhoeffer condemned this act as "heretical and contrary to the meaning of the Church." Bonhoeffer joined the Confessing Church and refused all compromise with the German-Christians. A member of the German delegation to the ecumenical conference at Fanö in Denmark, he gave a noted speech on peace on 28 August 1934.

In spring 1935, Bonhoeffer returned to Germany; entreated by the Confessing Church, he had accepted the principalship of the illegal theological seminary in Finkenwalde, near Stettin, which trained pastors for the Confessing Church. Bonhoeffer gave lectures on pastoral theology, preaching, teaching the catechism and the cure of souls. Equally, he inculcated in his seminarians a life of individual and community daily prayer, a process which he described in his *On Community Life* (1939).

In August 1936, Bonhoeffer was suspended from his teaching duties at the University of Berlin. A few months earlier, he had published an address from the Confessing Church to Hitler, declaring: "If according to the Nazi theory of the world Christians are obliged to adopt an anti-Semitism which makes hatred of the Jews compulsory, the Christian commandment of the love of neighbor will always oblige them to oppose this nonsense." In September 1937, the seminary at Finkenwalde was closed down on the orders of Heinrich Himmler. Bonhoeffer continued his work in secret, putting into practice the costly obedience to Christ which he explained in his *Nachfolge* (1937).

In 1939, Bonhoeffer left Germany again. After leaving Berlin in the beginning of June for a conference tour in the USA, he became consumed with remorse and returned to Germany in July in order to "share in these testing times with [his] people." In 1940, he was forbidden from speaking in public on any topic, and from writing anything readable by the public. With the support of his brother-in-law, Hans von Dohnanyi, he joined the counter-espionage service (the *Abwehr*), which allowed him, thanks to his ecumenical activities, to make contacts abroad (in Switzerland, Sweden and England) and to discover in these places the existence of a German resistance movement against Hitler.

In this way, during a trip to Sweden in 1942, he renewed his contact with the Anglican bishop George Bell, whom he had first met during his chaplaincy days in London. The two men sketched out peace projects for when Hitler had been eliminated, but they both failed to convince the Allies to offer military assistance to the German Resistance. These political activities did not prevent Bonhoeffer from continuing his theological work; he labored intensely on the editing of his *Ethics*, which was eventually published unfinished after his death.

On 13 January 1943, Bonhoeffer became engaged to Maria von Wedemeyer. But their joy was brief; on 5 April Bonhoeffer was arrested and imprisoned in Tegel military prison. Only after the failed attempt to assassinate Hitler on 20 July 1944 were solid links able to be proved between Bonhoeffer and the German Resistance — notably with one of the directors of the Abwehr, Admiral Wilhelm Canaris. Meanwhile, during months of solitary confinement, relieved occasionally by visits from members of his family, Bonhoeffer corresponded with Maria and with his student and friend Eberhard Bethge. After the war, Bethge published this correspondence. It is a collection of deeply moving letters, rich in theological insight. Far from standing detached from the problems of the German Church and society, in the isolation of his cell Bonhoeffer calmly foresaw the secularization which others were frightened to discover decades later — a world "come of age," "non-religious"; in this world, Bonhoeffer demanded that the faithful should not relegate God to a question of lip-service, but in their words and deeds should place him at the very center of all human existence.

After the military plot against Hitler of 20 July 1944, Bonhoeffer's prison conditions dramatically worsened. On 8 October, he was transferred to the notorious Gestapo prison on

Prinz-Albrecht-Strasse, after which he scarcely had any further contact with the outside world. On 7 February 1945, he was transferred to Buchenwald concentration camp. On 9 April 1945, after a parody of a trial, he was hanged at Flossenbürg concentration camp.

But his senseless death, less than a month before the end of the war, does not signify the defeat of faith. The camp doctor reported that, before being led to his death, Bonhoeffer prayed on his knees in his cell. The doctor was also struck by Bonhoeffer praying quietly again, as he climbed the steps leading to the noose. According to Bonhoeffer's prison companions, his last words were, "This is the end — but for me, the beginning of life"; they underline forcefully the hope of the gospel and bear witness to Bonhoeffer's trust in the faithfulness of God in and after death. Thanks to Eberhard Bethge, Bonhoeffer's words and ideas were not lost in that grey dawn in Flossenbürg. Published, then translated into many languages, his demanding message, centered on Christ, unceasingly proclaims that, whatever our personal circumstances, true freedom and true joy are given by God.

Introduction

*D*ietrich Bonhoeffer left us a good number of collections of prayers and reflections on prayer, several of which were published during his lifetime. Others — perhaps the best and most beautiful — were sent in secret to his friend Eberhard Bethge or to his fiancée Maria von Wedermeyer, and have been made public only recently. These prayers — written not in the comfort of a pastor's study but in a Nazi prison — are the most moving.

These prison prayers constitute the second half of this book (from Day 7 to Day 15), with Bonhoeffer's final poem *The Forces of Goodness* used for the last two days. We have not arranged the prayers chronologically, but have allowed Bonhoeffer to dictate a course of prayer for us.

Prayer is conversation with God. For Bonhoeffer, this prayer is addressed to the God revealed in Jesus Christ (Day 1). Why is this unusual for a Christian theologian? Because many Protestants in Bonhoeffer's day had

replaced the God of the Bible with a very different God of the Nation. Prayer is as natural
to the Christian as breathing (Day 2). Christian
prayer is rooted in the Psalms (Day 3) as well
as in the prayers of Jesus (Day 4). Prayer is
both an intimate and hidden encounter (see Mt
6:6) and a communal adventure, for which a
regular pattern needs to be fixed (Day 5).

Day 6 introduces the prison prayers, insisting
on the high price to be paid for walking the way
of Christ. Holding fast to God on behalf of all
humanity, and in opposition to pagan selfishness, is the distinctively Christian way (Day 7).
Christians remain in solidarity with the people of
Israel, to whom God will keep his promises (Day
8). For his unchurched cellmates, Bonhoeffer
wrote prayers which they could easily address to
God in the morning (Day 9), in the evening (Day
10), or in times of distress (Day 11).

In Bonhoeffer's personal encounter with
God, he asked himself questions about his own
identity — questions posed by God's existence
(Day 12) and questions which were rooted in
Bonhoeffer's past (Day 13). Surrounded in spirit
by all the individuals whom they love (Day 14),
the faithful can, in spite of present sufferings and
the threat of death, maintain confidence in God.
It is God who accompanies the believer morning
and evening, and who stays by him or her until
the last (Day 15).

Translator's Note

Translations of citations of Dietrich Bonhoeffer are either by me or, when marked "Bonhoeffer (English)", from *Dietrich Bonhoeffer, Letters and Papers from Prison (Abridged edition), London, SCM Press, 2001*. Biblical verses are from the Revised Standard Version. It has been a great privilege to translate this work of Professor Arnold on the great Twentieth-century prophet Dietrich Bonhoeffer, and all errors in understanding and translation are solely mine.

Jack McDonald
Cambridge, England 2008

1
Where Is Your God?

Focus Point

////////////

Bonhoeffer sets himself up against the prevailing tendencies of German Christian theology. He does not see God as active in German nationalism, and so distances himself from the Nazis. Nor does he follow the Nazis' chief theological opponent, Karl Barth, in seeing God as active only in the past. Bonhoeffer sees God as working through Jesus Christ in our day.

////////////

These things I remember,
as I pour out my soul:
how I went with the throng,
and led them in procession to the house of God,
with glad shouts and songs of thanksgiving,
a multitude keeping festival.

(Ps 42:4)

Where is your God? That is what they ask us in tones either worried, doubting or mocking. They see death, sin, misery, war, but they can also see bravery, strength and honor. But where is God? No one should be ashamed of the tears which flow because God is not yet to be seen and because we cannot show him to our neighbors. These are tears shed for God, tears which God recognizes (Ps 56:8). Where is your God? How do we reply, except by pointing towards the man who in his life, in his death and in his resurrection, showed himself the true Son of God: Jesus Christ? In death, he is our life; in sin, he is our forgiveness; in distress, he comes to help us; in war, he is our peace. As Luther says, "You should point to this man and say of him: there is God."

Lord Jesus, when I am tested, because in this world I can see neither the power of God nor his love, make me look with confidence to you; for you are my Savior and my God. Amen.

(Brevier 204)

//////////////

"So where is your God?" The question asked of the psalmist, who in turn asks it of him to whom he prays, resonated unceasingly and insistently throughout the four decades of Dietrich Bonhoeffer's life. When he was just a child, Germany (for the most part Protestant) had already paid a heavy tribute to secularization: confronted by the well-to-do ranks of their parishioners, the city clergy had begun to accept — without outlining any solution — that the church had failed to connect with the laboring classes. But in August 1914, many ministers believed that the answer to the question "Where is your God?" had at last arrived: surely God revealed himself in history as the God of Germany and of the Germans; God was indisputably and solely the German God, who sided with his people against foreign powers, in order to secure a German victory. In addition, this national-triumphant God was also the master of nature, who unleashed the elements to conquer his adversaries: "By means of thunder and lightning, and bombs and grenades, God brings to naught whatever resistance is offered to his high designs" (from a Church sermon of 1915). God's character was not compassion, mercy and love, but virility, force (indeed, brutality) and the exclusive care of his own.

The length and deadliness of the First World War led theologians to alter this image of God, and to call to mind an essential aspect of the Creator, that he is not reducible to an instrument of human hatred, but is sovereign over all. However, the mysterious and hidden God, both enticing and terrifying, who was rediscovered at the end of the First World War, borrowed these character-traits as much from Eastern and tribal religions as from the Bible. It is notable that Rudolf Otto, who defended this view in 1917, preferred to speak of "the Holy" or "the Holy One" (*das Heilige*) rather than directly of "God."

For the theologian Karl Barth (1886-1968), who refused to restrict God to one camp or the other (In a sermon of 27 December 1917, he said, "We have seen that God is something completely different from what self-styled Christianity has made him into. Everywhere, they have made gods to bless their arms of death, gods obliged to hate and to fight by their side."), God had embroiled himself in human history only in the past, in Jesus Christ. But this assertion, made to combat any false revelation of God, seemed to risk digging an unbridgeable divide between the Creator and his creatures now.

In the 1920s and 1930s, a few German theologians developed the idea that God revealed himself through "great men." Thus in 1933, they were able to interpret the arrival of Adolf Hitler as a divine act, which before their eyes brought to pass the restoration of Germany: "Our churches have greeted the turning-point in Germany of 1933 as a gift and a miracle from God" (Paul Althaus). Rare were the theologians far-seeing enough to recognize that Hitler, far from being a divine miracle, would plunge his country and a good part of the world into the abyss.

Bonhoeffer had been deeply struck by the First World War — in 1918, his brother Walter, seven years older, died from war wounds — and he spent the 1920s considering the Treaty of Versailles particularly unfair on Germany. However, thanks to his deepening engagement with both Testaments of the Bible, along with the literature of the Reformation, he began to refuse to see God where the majority of his countrymen chose to see him. He chose instead another way, by returning to the theology of Martin Luther: "I do not know any other God in heaven or earth than the one who speaks and acts towards me as I see and hear him in Christ" (Luther, *Weimarer Ausgabe,* vol. 45). In company with the great Reformer, to whom he explicitly acknowledged his debt, Bonhoeffer was able to reject any false notion of power, even the notion of the love of God, if it was a false one — a delicate area where Christians have not ceased to be confused.

In 1914, German clergy, emboldened and made desperate by the decline of religion, fell over themselves to confuse nationalist fervor and the renewal of the Faith; and for several years the clergy contributed to this confusion in word and deed. In 1933, humiliated still further by the Treaty of Versailles and by economic collapse, the German people were happy to see a foul-mouthed tin-pot warmonger as the prophet of Almighty God. So it was that twenty years on, they had fallen victim to the same tragic error, that of making God in their own image.

For Bonhoeffer, in the tradition of Karl Barth, God did not so much give human thoughts and feelings his seal of approval as put them in question: "In sin, God is our forgiveness; in distress, he is the one who comes to our aid; in war, he is our peace." But in opposition to what Barth taught after the First World War, Bonhoeffer did not restrict the revelation of Jesus Christ to the past — it is also *now* that God gives himself to be known in Christ, the one who triumphs over death, who forgives, who comforts and gives peace.

This rediscovery of the theology of the Cross has implications for prayer. Bonhoeffer prays that God will turn his sight towards Jesus Christ when he finds himself in time of trial. The gap between the fragile and embattled situation of the believer and his yearnings can lead him to doubt either the power or the love of God; indeed, how do we explain the absence of relief, if not by admitting that God is either feeble or cruel? But to remind oneself that God is the God revealed in Jesus Christ allows us to ask the question of theodicy differently, by changing our understanding of the purpose and content of prayer. On the one hand, Jesus Christ reveals the power of the love of God. And for the Christian, Jesus alone reveals this power. He assures human beings that the one who has shared their condition, even unto death, is not hostile to them, nor simply above them (like an idle God enthroned remotely on high), but with them and by their side. On the other hand, all prayer addressed to the Father models itself on the prayer Jesus taught to his disciples: the Lord's Prayer begins by praise of God's name, prayer for the coming of God's kingdom, and submission to the fulfillment of God's will.

Reflection Questions

How tempting is it to see God as favoring your nation? If God is omnipotent, why does Bonhoeffer say that God is not known in strength but in weakness? How much do you think Bonhoeffer follows a "theology of the Cross"? Why did Bonhoeffer so implacably despise Nazism?

2
Making Your Whole Life a Prayer

Focus Point

////////////

Bonhoeffer writes on the centrality of prayer in Christian life, and of God as our truest and deepest confidant.

////////////

The force of the human being is prayer. From your youth, familiarize yourself with prayer. To pray is to breathe alongside God. To pray is to give your life to God and to dedicate it to him. To pray is to place your trust in God.

When you get ready for bed in the evening, join your hands, instill a deep silence in yourself, and ask God to come close by. Then tell him how you have passed your day, whether you have made it holy or spoiled it. Tell him if you have passed the day with love or with anger, with peace or with hatred, in doing good or in doing evil, in purity or in profanity.

Then pray that God will make your soul holy and pure. Then be ashamed of the evil (which you have done), and be glad at the good (which you have done). Finally, before the eyes of God, name those who love you, thank God for giving you your father and your mother, for giving you the friends who love you, and pray to God to stay with all of them.

If you have something which you do not wish to confide with anyone, trust that God sees all things and knows all things. Go to him; and, at night, when all is calm and asleep, pour out your troubled heart to him, and he will give you rest. My dear child … do not forget: it is through prayer that you will become strong.

(DWB 10. 544f)

///////////////

At the beginning of 1928, just after Bonhoeffer had passed his first ordination examinations, he accepted an offer to work for a year as chaplain to the German community in Barcelona, the Catalan capital. In Spain, he busied himself particularly with developing activities for children, beginning with youth services — the congregations quickly rose to forty, and the children were so enthused by their young pastor that the youth services were well-attended even during the summer holidays.

Bonhoeffer made a point of visiting the parents of the children and teenagers who came to his youth groups, and the adults in their turn began to attend services. In addition, he began a successful religious studies course for the senior pupils of the German School in Barcelona; welcoming these pupils for weekly discussion evenings, Bonhoeffer also endeavored to help them with their schoolwork if necessary.

In his correspondence with his brother-in-law, Pastor Walter Dress, the young chaplain expressed the "great joy" which these youth liturgies gave him. He rejoiced that the children "were very confident and truly free in their relations with adults" (DWB 17. 72). He also reported to Dress in moving terms about how he had met a boy of ten years, troubled by the death of his pet dog:

> "Don't you see that God has made human beings and animals, and he certainly loves animals; and I believe that God takes all those which are loved on earth, which are truly loved, and gathers them around him, and they live with him. Because love is part of God's nature. But of course we don't know how this happens." You should have seen the joy which lit up this boy's face. (DWB 17. 83)

If Bonhoeffer invested so much effort in his youth work, it was not just because of his professional desire to increase the size of his congregation, nor even just because his own young age

— he was only twenty-two — drew him closer to children than to his colleagues and other adults. His labors were a response to deeper theological issues: Jesus directed himself towards children, as Bonhoeffer recalled insistently during a conference in Barcelona, *Jesus Christ and the Essence of Christianity* (DWB 10. 312f).

It is noteworthy that when Bonhoeffer took his second ordination examination on his return to Germany, his specimen example of a service of youth worship only just passed, for the reason that its content was judged over the heads of children. No doubt the examiners did not know that experience was on Bonhoeffer's side — he had no fear of discussing difficult questions with children and young people.

Bonhoeffer's thoughts on prayer, written for one of his pupils, come at the end of several pages of spiritual guidance concerning joy, purity and maturity, work and solitude. Touching this last theme, Bonhoeffer gave the young boy advice which he would take up again a decade later in his *On Community Life* (see Day 5): a daily time of solitary meditation was required, whether for thinking of the day to come or to review the day which has passed; it was also necessary to make God the guest of these "solitary hours," because he alone knows those things which do not leave our lips (DWB 10. 544).

Put simply, Bonhoeffer reveals to his protégé how vital prayer is, he offers an approach to prayer, and he then develops the content of this confident trust in God: repentance, request for holiness, thanksgiving and intercession. In an age when we are filled with self-doubt at the very same time that we constantly try to affirm our own personalities, it is crucial to hear someone say: It is God who gives you life, breath and force; it is the quality of your relations with him which will, above anything else, guide your personality. But this message does not only apply to children and young people. In different terms, but without compromising the message, Bonhoeffer did not cease to offer it to many and varied audiences. He did yet more: right up to his own death, when he breathed his last in God's company, he spent his life in prayer.

Reflection Questions

Why did Bonhoeffer not simplify complex theological ideas when organizing youth liturgies in Barcelona? "Pie in the sky when you die"? — On what basis did Bonhoeffer claim that animals have an existence in eternity? Why does this chapter on prayer also concern young people?

3

Praising God
with the Psalms

Focus Point

Bonhoeffer courts controversy with his fellow-Christians in Germany by basing his prayer-life on the Book of Psalms, as teaching us in turn about creation, law and salvation.

I say to God, my rock, "Why have you forgotten me? Why must I walk about mournfully because the enemy oppresses me?" (Ps 42:9)

How long and disheartening both day and night are when we are without God. But how joyful even the worst day becomes when I manage to graft the goodness of God onto it and when I trust that all things work together for good for those who love God. And how calm and healing becomes the deepest night when I mark it by song and prayer to God, the God of my life. The promises of God are true every day and every night, and they fill every day and every night, week on week, year on year. All I need do is claim them.

O God the Holy Spirit, fulfill in me all your promises. I am ready, day and night. Fill me wholly. Amen.

(Brevier 209)

///////////////

*B*y praying with the Book of Psalms — "this work of Holy Scripture which stands out from all the other biblical books by the fact that it only contains prayers" (DWB 5. 108) — Bonhoeffer acted in a very conventional Christian tradition. He equally put into practice the instructions of the Apostle Paul, which were very familiar to him (see *On Community Life* [1939], DWB 5. 38) — "Say the psalms together" (see Eph 5:19) and "Teach yourselves and encourage yourselves with the psalms" (see Col 3:16).

However, in the Germany of his day, where Protestant monastic communities were rare, where certain Protestants wanted to deny the canonical validity of the Old Testament and where others were demanding the "dejudification" of the Bible, Bonhoeffer's position did not go without saying. Still more difficult and courageous was to publish, in 1940, an introduction to the Psalms, under the title *The Prayer Book of the Bible*.

In this little work, Bonhoeffer celebrates the fact that many Churches have maintained the "immeasurable riches" of singing or reading the Psalms liturgically (see DWB 5. 115). With Martin Luther (*Preface to the Neuburg Psalter*, 1545), Bonhoeffer insisted on the legitimacy of these strong-minded prayers. He invited Christians not to gravitate towards "lighter fare," but to reject this in favor of a regular and deep reading of the Psalter: once we are accustomed to the Psalter, we tend not to bother with our own words in prayer, finding them tepid and insipid (see DWB 5. 115).

To those communities which were no longer familiar with the practice of reading the Psalter — Bonhoeffer was thinking primarily of Christians in Germany — he recommended the daily reading of and meditation upon several psalms. In this way, they would read the Book of Psalms several times each year, and would be able to steadily delve into it more deeply. He recalled the extent to which the Psalter had filled the life of the Early Church, how much it had marked the daily lives of Church Fathers such as Jerome, and above all, how verses from the Psalms had been spoken by Jesus on the cross.

By abandoning the Psalms, a Christian community loses a unique treasure; but when it rediscovers them, it receives unimagined strength. (DWB 5. 116)

In Finkenwalde Seminary (see Day 5 in this book), Bonhoeffer arranged matters to begin each day with a meditation centered on prayer from the Psalms:

The Psalter is the greatest school of prayer. We learn from it first and foremost what prayer means: prayer is grounding itself and us in the Word of God; prayer is grounding us in the divine promises.... We also learn from the prayers in the Psalms what we should pray about. (DBW 5. 40 — *On Community Life*)

Whether they express a plea or whether they are an aid to doctrine, in the end all the Psalms are hymns, composed to celebrate the glory of God (see DWB 5. 113). The various great themes which Bonhoeffer distinguishes in the Psalms are all linked to the praise of God — first, *creation*, which invites us to celebrate God's power and his many gifts, and also his grace-filled action towards humanity; secondly, *law*, whose joyful character is expressed in the Psalms, since it offers precepts designed for a structured life (unlike many theologians of the period, Bonhoeffer did not set Law [as linked to the Old Testament] in opposition to Grace [as central to the message of Jesus]) — "In us, Jesus thanks the Father for the grace and law, and, by what he accomplished, Jesus offers us joy" (DWB 5. 118f); thirdly, *salvation*, which is seen in history from the Exodus right up to Calvary.

Bonhoeffer especially lingered on the requests for life and happiness so frequent in the Psalms. In the light of the cross of Christ, certain Christians considered that earthly blessings should never be the object of prayer, and preferring to be "more spiritual than God himself" (DBW 5. 122), they viewed the Psalmist's requests as evidence of a defective faith which had been corrected by the New Testament. Bonhoeffer had none of this: the Psalmist's requests were of the same order as those in the Lord's Prayer for daily bread, which were addressed to the God "who created and maintains this life" (DWB 5. 123). If God has given us these "worldly" prayers, it is "to enable us the better to know him, praise him and love him" (DBW 5. 123). One year earlier, in *On Community Life*, Bonhoeffer complained that "we prevent God from giving us the great spiritual gifts which he has prepared for us, because we do not thank him for his small, daily gifts" (DBW 5. 25).

But doesn't the cross, together with the disciplines demanded of those who follow Christ, undermine these Psalm prayers? Doesn't the cross reveal their vacuity? For Bonhoeffer, the

very opposite was true — assuming that we are
mindful of the teaching of Psalm 37:16, "Better
is a little that the righteous person has than the
abundance of many wicked." Therefore, to pray
for worldly goods, the gifts of the Creator, comes
down in the end to asking him to stay in communion with us. It is this which is the highest
and most valuable gift which he grants to those
who ask.

God offers and keeps this communion when
material goods are removed from us — paradoxi-
cally, it is in such circumstances that God draws
closest to us. Through deprivation and spiritual
discipline, God prepares believers to win eternal
life, once death has severed all attachment to
the world (see DWB 5. 123). Prayer for worldly
goods does not contradict this preparation; it
contributes towards it:

> Because of Jesus Christ, and by reason
> of his command alone, we have the right
> to pray for the things which are essential
> to life; and it is because of him that we
> should do this with confidence. But when
> we receive what we need, we should not
> cease to give thanks to God with all our
> hearts for displaying such graces in Jesus
> Christ. (DWB 5. 123)

Reflection Questions

Do you agree with Bonhoeffer that "the Psalter is the greatest school of prayer"? How far do you agree with Bonhoeffer that regular prayer with spiritual texts like the Psalms makes spontaneous prayer seem superficial and shallow? Even though Bonhoeffer thought that we should pray for material benefits, why in the end does he seem to say that we shouldn't, for example, pray for a new car? Is God closer when we have nothing?

4
Praying Thanks to Jesus Christ

Focus Point

////////////

Bonhoeffer bases all his ability to pray on standing alongside Jesus Christ and praying as he taught us. The Lord's Prayer is the touchstone of all Christian prayer.

////////////

"Lord, teach us to pray ..." (Lk 11:1). This is what the disciples said to Jesus. In doing this, they revealed themselves to be incapable of praying. They needed to learn. "Learning to pray" seems a contradiction to us. We would say either, "our hearts overflow until they begin to pray by themselves" or, "our hearts will never learn to pray." But herein lies the dangerous error — albeit common in

50

today's Christianity — of thinking that our hearts can learn to pray naturally. Here we confuse desire, hope, sighing, beseeching and joy (all of which our hearts can achieve by themselves) with praying (which they can't). And so we confuse the earth with heaven, and mankind with God. [But] to pray is not simply to open one's heart. It is to find there — whether the heart is overflowing or empty — the way which leads to God, and to speak with him there. This can be done by no one by himself. Human beings need Jesus Christ to do it....

Christ wishes to pray with us. We can make his prayer our own, and it is because of this that we can be sure and joyful that God hears us. When our will and our whole heart enter into the prayer of Christ, then we truly pray. And it is only in Jesus Christ the Word that we can pray; and it is only in him that we will be heard.

(DWB 5. 107)

////////////

*I*n 1933, Bonhoeffer gave a class on "What and who is Jesus Christ?" Despite what such a title might make us expect, the questions posed by Bonhoeffer here related less to the past (exhuming the historical Jesus) than to the present — how do we recognize Jesus Christ as the Lord of all, as the first disciples did? Then in 1937, in his *Nachfolge*, literally meaning "Follow [Jesus]" or "Walk in the steps [of Jesus]," Bonhoeffer developed the theme of the costly call given by Jesus to his disciples in all ages to follow him in the way of obedience. Over the few pages of this book dedicated to "the hidden character of prayer," Bonhoeffer gives a commentary on Matthew 6:5–8, where Jesus invites his listeners to pray in secret and without heaping up empty phrases.

Bonhoeffer begins by reminding us that it is Jesus who teaches his disciples to pray. Prayer is not a right in the eyes of God just because it consists in "a natural need of the human heart" (DWB 4. 157); rather, "the disciples have the right to pray because it is Jesus, the one who knows the Father, who tells them to" (DWB 4. 157). Bonhoeffer therefore conceives of prayer as an act of obedience to Jesus. He also insists on the necessity of Christ as the mediator of our prayer: through him alone, Christians can discover the Father.

What is the link between these thoughts of Bonhoeffer and the sayings of Jesus concerning the hypocrites who "have already received their reward" (see Mt 6:2)? The hypocrites have transformed themselves into spectators of their own prayer; they have listened only to themselves, and are quite satisfied at having done so. They therefore have their reward in the answered prayer which they have accorded to themselves. God will give them no other satisfaction than the self-publicity which they have performed (see DBW 4. 158f).

On the other hand, those whose prayer flows from the will of Jesus will avoid this narcissistic gossip, and will discover the living God. In the same manner, they will leave to God the care of answering their prayer. Through the Lord's Prayer and in himself, Jesus taught his follow-ers — and therefore has taught Christians in all ages — "the *way* in which they should pray, and *what* they should pray" (DBW 4. 160).

As an introduction to *The Bible's Prayer-book: an Introduction to the Psalms* (1940), Bonhoeffer based his theories on the other Gospel which contains the Lord's Prayer, St. Luke's. He begins with the request, addressed by the dis-ciples to their master, "Lord, teach us to pray" (Lk 11:1). Prayer, he insists, is not natural to human beings; rather it requires training. The Christian resembles, next to God, a small child whose father is teaching him to talk. In order to have a conversation with God, the heavenly Father, the child must first learn his father's language. He begins simply by repeating his Father's words.

Bonhoeffer rejects false spontaneity in prayer — "the untrustworthy and random language of our hearts" — and prefers "the clear and pure language in which God has spoken to us in Jesus Christ" (DBW 5. 108). This is the language which we encounter in the Holy Scriptures. It is this language which should become the foundation of our prayer, in order that the words which have come from God will become "the steps by which we will find God" (DBW 5. 108). Bonhoeffer goes further by wondering if it isn't essential, in order to pray correctly, to pray "against our own heart":

> It isn't the fact that we want to pray which is important, but the reason for which God wants us to pray. If we lean only on ourselves, without a doubt we often end up praying just the fourth petition of the Lord's Prayer. But God wishes otherwise. It isn't the poverty of our heart but the riches of the Word of God which should shape our prayer. (DBW 5. 109)

Bonhoeffer identifies the danger of prayer which consists simply in outpourings towards God, or which is limited to requests for material benefit. Prayer like this omits the first three petitions of the Lord's Prayer, which give a definite shape to all requests by Christians for themselves. Anything which departs from this shape, says Bonhoeffer brusquely, isn't a prayer (DBW 5. 109).

In a traditional fashion, Bonhoeffer paints the Lord's Prayer as the prayer which encapsulates all prayer, and the prayer which summarizes and crowns all the prayers of the Bible. (In *Nachfolge*, he had qualified it as "the prayer *par excellence*....") The Lord's Prayer is not an example of the prayer of the disciples; rather, we *must* pray as Jesus has taught us" (DBW 4. 160). It is also — and here Bonhoeffer pursues his warning against the risk of confusing human speech and the words of or wished by God — "the touchstone prayer, allowing us to determine if we are praying in the name of Jesus Christ or in our own name" (DBW 5. 109). Even so, Bonhoeffer does not conceive of the Lord's Prayer as an idol, but as the simple guarantee of the certainty that those who pray it will be heard by God (DBW 4. 160).

Certainly, other passages in Bonhoeffer (for example, see Day 5 in this collection) show that for Bonhoeffer prayer is *also* the unburdening of our own hearts. But it is never only this, and indeed never primarily this — prayer first and foremost implies that we open ourselves to a word from outside ourselves, the better to begin a real dialogue.

Reflection Questions

Why, for Bonhoeffer, is prayer not a human right but an act of Christian obedience? According to Bonhoeffer, how do we avoid "narcissistic gossip" when we pray? Do you agree with Bonhoeffer that praying against our own hearts' wishes is generally a sign of authentic prayer? Why is the first half of the Lord's Prayer more important for Bonhoeffer than the second half?

5
Praying in Church

Focus Point

///////////

Bonhoeffer outlines a blueprint for a new monasticism in which individual Christians come together
as a foretaste of the perfect community of heaven.

///////////

> *Why are you cast down, O my soul, and*
> *why are you disquieted within me?*
> *Hope in God; for I shall again praise him,*
> *my help and my God.*
>
> *(Ps 42:5)*

> *I am alone. There is no one to whom I can*
> *unburden my heart. So I do this to myself*
> *and before the God to whom I cry. It is good*
> *to unburden your heart in solitude and not*
> *to live with the aftertaste of your grief. But*
> *the more I am alone, the more I have the*

desire to be connected to other Christians, to worship together, to pray, to sing, to praise, to give thanks and to celebrate together. I call this communion to mind, and the love I have for it grows within me. Those who cry to God cry to Jesus Christ, and those who cry to Jesus Christ cry to the Church.

O God the Holy Spirit, give me brothers with whom I may be in communion in faith and in prayer, with whom I may carry all [the burdens] which are laid on me. Bring me home to your Church, to your Word and to your Holy Supper. Amen.

(Brevier 205)

///////////

P rotestant Christianity has always insisted on the truth of a trusting and mature face-to-face encounter between the believer and the Creator. However, this is not to diminish the role of common prayer: Bonhoeffer is part of the great company of Protestant theologians who, ever since Luther, have insisted — in spite of the temptations and distractions of an individualistic approach — on the importance of the local church, the community of believers gathered together to share Word and Sacrament. But Bonhoeffer did more: he tried to reintroduce a form of monasticism, open to the world, into the Protestant Church.

From the age of twenty-two, when he began his chaplaincy in Barcelona, Bonhoeffer alternated periods devoted to study and teaching with those dedicated to leading a parish. His years spent in England (1933–1935) were formative in Bonhoeffer's discovery of the monastic life in Anglican and Free Church communities. Thanks to Bishop George Bell, Bonhoeffer was able to visit a number of Anglican monasteries refounded according to the Benedictine Rule — notably the Community of the Resurrection in Mirfield, Yorkshire, and the Society of the Sacred Mission in Kelham. He also visited the Methodist College in Richmond and the Quaker Centre at Selly Oak in Birmingham. On 14 January 1935, he wrote to his brother Karl-Friedrich from London:

> The renewal of the Church will emerge from a new kind of monasticism, one with nothing in common with the old except a dogged following of life in the footsteps of Christ, shaped by the Sermon on the Mount. I think that the moment has come to call people together for this. (DWB 13. 273)

Bonhoeffer speaks of a "new kind of monasticism" because he never imagined the Christian community as an escape, sheltered from the world.

When, in 1935, Bonhoeffer accepted the post of Rector of Finkenwalde, this was at the expense of the prospect of a trip of several months in India. For several years beforehand, Bonhoeffer had hoped to meet Gandhi to deepen his understanding of non-violence. Because of his loyalty to the Confessing Church and because of his desire to shape the training of the clergy, Bonhoeffer abandoned learning at the feet of Gandhi in order to become in his own right a spiritual master to younger colleagues.

Bonhoeffer's work, *On Community Life*, published in 1939, reflects his experience of Finkenwalde Seminary, which he led from 1935 to 1937. The Confessing Church set up its own colleges to train clergy because the teaching offered in a number of university faculties of theology (the normal route to ordination) had become tainted by the antisemitic ideas of the German Christians. For Bonhoeffer, the theological training undertaken by the young pastors of the Confessing Church had to include community living — for theological and pastoral work to take root, they must be grafted into a life shaped by meeting every morning and evening around the Word, and by fixed times for prayer.

This framework for Christian life did not go without saying in the Church, and Bonhoeffer was obliged to respond with firmness to those who cast accusations of "legalism" at him, or who thought that time spent in meditation was a waste of time which could be spent learning how to catechize or to preach: "… this is a wholesale misunderstanding of what a young theologian today should be, or a criminal ignorance of how a catechism class or a sermon are born" (DBW 14. 237; in a letter to Karl Barth of 19 September 1936).

Fortunately, the young pastors who came to be taught at Finkenwalde — some of them had already experienced prison, and many of them had already been threatened, placed under pressure, or disadvantaged because of their opposition to the Nazi régime — did not share the reluctance of their elders. In the seminary of the Confessing Church, the day began with a meditation. Biblical readings consisted of a whole chapter from the Old Testament and a long extract from the New Testament. On Saturdays, Bonhoeffer would give an exposition of a biblical text. During the rest of the week, he would lead free prayer. These services ended with a hymn and a blessing. After breakfast, half-an-hour of private, silent meditation took place in students' rooms. Before lunch, half-an-hour was equally dedicated to hymn practice. The evening meditation mirrored what occurred in the morning. Holy Communion was celebrated once each month.

In *On Community Living*, Bonhoeffer defended the emphasis he placed on this community life, and explained the daily régime at Finkelwalde. In the present age, believers are spread about in the world, and waiting to be gathered together at the end of time; so when believers gather together for prayer and worship, they have a foretaste of the community of the end of time, in the Kingdom of God. It is therefore a grace-ful gift of God to be able even now to gather around the Word and the Sacraments. Because of this grace, believers respond with prayers of thanks.

In essence, all Christians need their broth-ers and sisters in Christ to give them strength and happiness; this Christian community announces the forgiveness and the grace of the Word of God, and so it allows the individual to draw close to Christ. In return, Christ urges all Christians to see one another as sister and brother, since Christ himself has smashed apart the isolation caused by selfishness. In this way, the visible community of believers, the body of Christ, can only be a community "through Christ and in Christ" (DBW 5. 21). The rules which govern community life all flow from this foundation.

To arrange one's day by including specific times of prayer is to recognize that all our time is given to us by God, the creator of time. Before our daily work, and even before our first meal, we should place the whole day under the sign of God: "It is only when the community is seized and strengthened by the bread of eternal life that it can gather together to receive from God the daily bread of this bodily life" (DBW 5. 56).

The morning is also the time when Christ's disciples wait for him — that is why this time of day belongs to the community, gathered in praise and recognition. Morning meditation consists of three elements: first, the Word of Scripture, which reveals God (see DBW 5. 44) and for which Bonhoeffer recommends a continuous reading, rather than the selection of preferred texts; then singing, "the voice of the Church which praises, gives thanks and makes requests" (DBW 5. 49); then common prayer, nourished by the Psalms. "Where Christians wish to live in common under the Word of God, it is equally in common that, in their own words, they must and can pray to God" (DBW 5. 53).

The time which follows is devoted to work: Bonhoeffer had truly taken to heart the instruction "ora et labora." Work does not distance Christians from God, because at work as much as anywhere else they encounter their Creator and serve their fellow men and women.

At noon, the community pauses briefly: when the day is half-spent, thanks are given to the Trinity, who is asked to keep the community safe until the evening.

Evening Prayer, which follows the same course as Morning Prayer, occurs right at the end of the day, so that the words of Evening Prayer are the last said before the repose of sleep. Once its human actions are performed, the community places itself back into the hands of God — "once we are overtaken by fatigue, it is God himself who will accomplish his work" (DBW 5. 62) — and commits to him all Christians, along with the poor, the sick and the lonely.

Bonhoeffer understands in a complementary way the relationship between times of common prayer (*der gemeinsame Tag*) and moments of private prayer (*der einsame Tag*), equally characterized by intercession and meditation on the Scriptures:

> We see this: it is only by finding ourselves in community that we can be alone; and it is only those who can be alone who can find themselves in community. (DBW 5. 66)

While he adopts many aspects of monastic life, Bonhoeffer is notable for distancing himself from much of the traditional content of monastery and convent life. At Finkenwalde, Bonhoeffer insisted that community life did not aim to be a separation or a retreat from the world, but an inner concentration in order to serve the world better (see DBW 14.

77). In effect, the small, local community of Finkenwalde considered itself just as a little part of the one, holy, catholic and Christian Church, whose pains, struggles and hopes it shared in action and in suffering (see DBW 5. 32).

This community life continued once the theological students had left the seminary. Bonhoeffer urged the "old boys" to visit one another, and to return to Finkenwalde during their holidays. When the constraints of war prevented them from meeting together, the former principal did not cease, through circulars, to maintain the mutual links among members of his community, inviting them to pray for one another. For Bonhoeffer, intercession was the living out of the love of one's neighbor. He knew that a pastor could not truly achieve his vocation without this support from his "brothers."

In 1942, Bonhoeffer continued to advise them to keep set times for prayer, for meditation and for the study of Scripture, and if possible to prepare their sermons together, in the context of prayer (see DBW 16. 588). This monastic discipline did not just support young clergy during the grim years of the Third Reich: as we shall see, it also helped Bonhoeffer to keep well during his two years of imprisonment.

Reflection Questions

Bonhoeffer said that the new monasticism would have nothing in common with the old "except a dogged following of life in the footsteps of Christ." What do you think Bonhoeffer considered essential to this new Christian monastic life? What do you think Bonhoeffer might have learned from Mahatma Gandhi had they actually met? How did Bonhoeffer think that the spiritual needs of individuals and communities could be met? How was the communal life of the Finkenwalde seminary an apt preparation for Bonhoeffer's imprisonment?

6
Called and
Conquered by God

Focus Point

////////////

Bonhoeffer turns his back on earthly rewards and seeks "endless insecurity," the better to appreciate the power of God in his life. This leads him to contemplate politically radical steps.

////////////

O Lord, you have enticed me, and I was enticed; you have overpowered me, and you have prevailed. I have become a laughingstock all day long; everyone mocks me. (Jer 20:7)

O God, it is you who have acted first with me. You have assiduously pursued me. You have never ceased to encounter me on my journey, here and there, unexpectedly. You have enticed and captivated me. You have made my heart obedient and docile. You have spoken of your burning desire and of your endless love, of your loyalty and your power. When I lacked strength, you gave me strength. When I yearned for support, you gave me support. When I looked for forgiveness, you forgave.

I did not want it, but you triumphed over my will, over my resistance and over my heart. O God, you seduced me irresistibly, so much so that I gave myself to you utterly. You took hold of me without my realizing it — and now I am incapable of letting go of you. You lead me along like the spoils of war. You yoke us to your triumphal chariot and you pull us along behind, so that … we may take our part in your triumphal procession. Could we ever have known that your love could be so exquisite and that your grace could be so strict?

You have become too strong for me, and you have triumphed. When your thought becomes strong in me, I become weak. When you turn towards me, I am lost: my will is broken, my strength is too feeble, and I must travel the way of suffering — I cannot retrace my steps: the decision which grips my life has already been taken. And it is not

*I who has decided: you have bound me to
yourself, for better, for worse.*

O God, why are you so terrifyingly close to us?
                                    (Brevier 300f)

//////////////

*T*his prayer, which takes up and develops
the dramatic tone of the confessions
of Jeremiah, expresses a theme very dear to
Bonhoeffer: to obey God's call and to follow
Jesus Christ as a result, has a price. The road
traveled by the believer is not a gentle stroll: as
the prophet Jeremiah has it, those who declare
the Word of God will see their will "crushed"
by the Creator, at the same time as they encounter the inevitable opposition of their neighbors.

Bonhoeffer himself endured this unhappy
experience. On several occasions, he had the
opportunity to leave Hitler's Germany for
good, and so to escape the fate doled out to the
opponents of the Nazi régime. As pastor of the
German Church in London from 1933 to 1935,
Bonhoeffer would have been able to choose to
stay in England, or else — to follow his own ear-
nestly expressed desire — to go to India to meet
Gandhi and to learn from him about non-violent
resistance. But he accepted instead the challenge
of founding and leading the theological college
of the Confessing Church at Finkenwalde.

After being dismissed from his post at the University of Berlin, and after watching powerless as the State closed the seminary at Finkenwalde, Bonhoeffer returned to London, and then, in the spring of 1939, accepted a lectureship in the United States. However, after just a few weeks, he went back to Germany: "I will not have the right to take part in the reconstruction of the Christian life of Germany after the war if I do not now share the current trials with my people" (DBW 15. 210: letter to Reinhold Niebuhr at end of June or beginning of July 1939).

Recruited to the counter-espionage service by his brother-in-law Hans von Dohnanyi, Bonhoeffer did not allow himself to benefit from the advantages of this post, which spared him from military service, and so from the requirement to kill. Using his ecumenical networks, he dedicated himself to forging links with the German opposition to Hitler abroad. Without being fully implicated in the attempts on Hitler's life, he nonetheless suffered the same fate as those who were judged with him: in October 1944, he abandoned an escape plan in order not to worsen the situation of his fellow prisoners and to spare his family from reprisals.

This "path towards Resistance," as Bonhoeffer's biographers have termed it, cannot be seen as the direct journey of a man who never harbored doubt or fear. Nor is it the path of a confident martyr who deliberately places himself in danger and seeks death. Bonhoeffer's life was full of twists and turns, full of choices, which Bonhoeffer never took lightly. It is because of this that Bonhoeffer can quite rightly speak of God's initiative, of the triumph of God's will over his own, of God's timeless decisions engaging with his own life, even of God's "tough grace."

To understand the apparent contradiction of this "tough grace," we must dwell on the remarkable words of Bonhoeffer in his *The Price of Grace* (1937 — also see Day 4 above), which he wrote while still Rector of Finkenwalde. In it, he traces accurately the insecurity for the Confessing Church and its clergy which would result from their opposition to Nazi religious policy. But could Bonhoeffer have imagined that a few years later he would pay for his opposition to Hitler first with his liberty and then with his life? In any case, *The Price of Grace* does not flinch from drawing the ultimate consequences of the deep obedience demanded by the living God:

> ... Disciples must conquer their fear of death by means of their fear of God. The danger for the disciple is not the judgment of men but the judgment of

God, not the loss of the body but the eternal loss of body and soul. Those who fear men do not fear God. Those who fear God have no need to fear men. (DBW 4. 208)

The grace which cost God dear — the life of his Son — is hardly likely to be cut-price for those who have been "bought at a high price" (see 1 Pt 1:18–19). Obedience to Jesus, which involves belonging to him, leads to abandoning all that human beings possess. In opposition to his contemporaries, Bonhoeffer refused to give the radical commands of Jesus a veneer which diminished their bluntness: Jesus' commands do not require just an internal response (for example, to keep our wealth in tranquility, but to live as if we did not have it); they demand a "straightforward [outward] obedience." As Bonhoeffer puts it, "It is only in solid obedience that mankind becomes liberated in his faith" (DWB 4. 73).

In his lifetime, Bonhoeffer was among those rare examples who undertook to "burn their bridges" and to "take a step in the direction of endless insecurity, in order to be able to see what Jesus is asking and what he is giving" (DWB 4. 51). He dared to experience this total encounter with Christ, which demanded the whole person unconditionally; he made that step confident in Jesus' call, in order to experience the truth that this call was "a more solid ground than all the world's securities" (DWB 4. 69).

Bonhoeffer never disguised the difficulties of this level of obedience, nor the evident suffering of the cross "prepared for all from the beginning of their communion with Jesus Christ" (DWB 4. 81; see Mk 8:34). But Bonhoeffer equally affirmed and lived out the paradox of this communion with the one who was crucified: "To walk under this cross is not the misery and despair [which come from alienation from God], but a new vigor and solace for our souls.... Under his yoke we have the certainty of Christ's presence and his communion" (DWB 4. 84).

Reflection Questions

Why for Bonhoeffer is God "terrifyingly close"? What motivated Bonhoeffer to return to Germany — and to certain persecution — at the start of World War II? Bonhoeffer never courted martyrdom, but what view did he have of the place of Christ's cross in Christian life?

7
Christians and Pagans

Focus Point

////////////

Bonhoeffer summarizes Christian salvation in the simplest of terms: God does not satisfy human desires; God is known in Christ in weakness and failure; God feeds us with the bread of his broken body.

////////////

Men go to God when they are sore bestead,
Pray to him for succour, for his peace,
    for bread,
For mercy for them sick, sinning, or dead;
All men do so, Christian and unbelieving.

Men go to God when he is sore bestead,
Find him poor and scorned, without
    shelter or bread,

Whelmed under weight of the wicked,
  the weak, the dead;
Christians stand by God in his hour of
  grieving.

God goes to every man when sore bestead,
Feeds body and spirit with his bread;
For Christians, pagans alike he hangs dead,
And both alike forgiving.

                    (Henkys 134)
           (Bonhoeffer [English] 131)

//////////////

*O*n 8 July 1944, a little while before the failed attempt on Hitler's life which would seal his own fate, Bonhoeffer wrote the shortest of his poems, *Christians and Pagans,* in a letter to his friend Eberhard Bethge. On first reading, these three verses of four lines each do not seem to be a prayer at all — there is no speech in the first person, no address to God in the second person, no linguistic signal of a dialogue with the Creator, nor any request, lament, query, praise or thanksgiving offered to God.

And yet this text, moving in its plainness, is entirely concerned with the relations between God and humans (*Menschen*), Christians (*Christen*) and pagans (*Heiden*). In short phrases and in simple terms which studiously avoid any religious vocabulary (except for the term "sin"), Bonhoeffer offers a gripping summary of the history of salvation.

He begins by describing humanity at prayer (verse 1): this prayer is a simple request for help, whether material ("bread") or spiritual ("happiness"). However, this happiness is not the joy which God gives, but the basic fact of being content because all one's wishes are fulfilled. Without passing judgment, Bonhoeffer describes this customary religious attitude, which consists in seeing God solely as the dispenser of happiness or the comforter in times of distress — that is, someone whose main task is to satisfy human desire. This approach belongs to those who in their everyday life take God but lightly, but it also relates to Christians: Bonhoeffer had just described in a letter to Bethge both the process of secularization ("the fact that God has been expelled from the world, beyond the public domain of human living," DBW 8. 509) and the hopeless attempts of some of the clergy to smuggle God back in "fraudulently" (DBW 8. 511), as being among the weaknesses of humanity.

Bonhoeffer's own perspective asserts itself in the second verse, where people encounter the God of paradox revealed in Jesus Christ: those around Jesus were waiting for him expectantly in triumph, but found him in unhappiness and humiliation. As a result, most of those around Jesus rejected him, and only the true Christians stayed, suffering, at his side. It is this gesture which distinguishes them from pagans. Bonhoeffer hints at this in this poem, before openly stating it four days later in his letters to Bethge of 16 and 18 July 1944:

> Here is the crucial difference between Christianity and all religion. Human religious feeling propels us in our distress to the power of God seen in the universe, God is the *deus ex machina*. But the Bible propels mankind to the weakness and the suffering of God. Only the suffering God is any use to us. (DWB 8. 534)

> "Christians keep near to God in their suffering." Here we see what distinguishes Christians from pagans. "Can you not watch with me one hour?" says Jesus at Gethsemane. It is the opposite of everything which the religious man expects from God. Mankind is called to suffer with God the particular suffering which a world without God inflicts on God. (DWB 8. 535)

"To keep oneself with God": This expression, Bonhoeffer explained on 10 August 1944, "comes without doubt from the thought of the Cross" (DWB 5. 562). Bonhoeffer was thinking of the Crucifixion, marked by the desertion of many and by the loyal presence of a few women — "Near the cross of Jesus were his mother, and his mother's sister, Mary the wife

of Clopas, and Mary Magdalene" (Jn 19:25).
Bonhoeffer's poem also shows the influence of
one of his favorite authors, Paul Gerhardt, and
the sixth verse of his famous song *The leader
covered in wounds* (*O Haupt voll Blut und Wunden*)
— "I want to keep myself near you...." These
few words are pregnant with meaning:

> It is not religious actions [separate from
> the world] which make the Christian,
> but sharing the suffering of God in the
> life of the world. This is what conversion
> (*metanoia*) is: not to think first of our own
> unhappiness, problems, sins and agonies,
> but to allow ourselves to be led on the
> way of Jesus Christ. (DWB 8. 535f)

After a year and a half in prison, Bonhoeffer
would have had plenty of opportunity to look
the "pagans" of his age up and down, beginning with the *Deutsche Christen*, the German
Protestants who aimed to marry Christianity
with Nazism, in the name of a God both German
and victorious. The Bonhoeffer who was paying
so dearly for his journey "on the way of Christ"
would have been able to construct his poem on
the entrenched opposition between popular religious feeling and authentic Christianity.

However, without denying this opposition, the final verse of Bonhoeffer's poem goes
beyond it and rejects all moralizing: to assume
the stance of the Pharisee of the parable in Luke

18:9-13 is to understand nothing at all of the God of the Passion. Although in the first two verses, the movement or motion goes from the human to the divine, this is reversed in the final verse: "God comes to all men…." Thus the perspective is broadened, at the same time as the paradox of "God in his misery" is resolved: it is with the riches of his bread — the bread of his broken body — that God nourishes body and soul; it is for humanity that he dies; it is by this death that he forgives them, saving them all from sin, from blame and from death.

God reveals himself as sovereign, while turning upside-down the assumptions of traditional religion: he "fulfills not all our desires, but all his promises: he remains the Lord of the world, which is now his Church; he offers us this faith again … he rejoices with us in his nearness and his support; he hears our prayers and leads us to himself through the best and most just way. In doing this faithfully, he merits our praise" (DBW 8. 569: letter of 14 August 1944).

So we see that the point of this poem of prayer is not to distinguish — nor indeed to separate — Christians from pagans. Rather than setting up one part of humanity against another, Bonhoeffer affirms that the God revealed in Jesus Christ wishes to remove this difference: "God comes to all men … and forgives one group as he forgives another." The second lesson given in these lines, underlined by leaving the initiative to

God in the final verse, is the call to a true life and to
true Christian prayer: not just to stay and remain
close to God in his Passion, but also to allow him
to come close to us. Christian life can only be an
active following of Jesus Christ because it is first
an acceptance of the gift of God.

When Bonhoeffer composed this, could he
have imagined that it would be set to music
and used as a communal prayer? The poem
"Christians and Pagans" was given a musical
setting in 1970 and was included in a hymn-book
three years later. In 1996, it was included in the
"Passion" section of the official hymn-book of
the Church of Wurtemberg.

Reflection Questions

If we are honest, how much of our own
prayer-life is directed to giving God a shopping-
list of personal requests? Is it unsettling for us
to hear Bonhoeffer speak of God poor and
scorned? The title "Christians and Pagans"
initially sounds like a traditional poem pointing
out the differences between these two groups.
How in fact does Bonhoeffer unite them? Why
for Bonhoeffer is God best seen through suffering?

8

Praying with Moses and the People of Israel

Focus Point

////////////

Bonhoeffer's sense of the Gospel compels him to take the side of the Jews persecuted and murdered by the Nazis, and to embrace openly the Old Testament and its hope for a Promised Land.

////////////

On the mountain-top, Moses stands, man
of God and prophet.
…
Moses prays: "Thus you accomplish, Lord,
what you have promised.
Never have you broken the promise which
you made to me.
Your blessings and your punishments have
always been directed aright.

You have saved us from slavery, and in
your arms you have embraced us.
Through desert and sea, you have won-
    drously gone before us.
The people's murmurs, cries and complaints
you have borne with total patience.
…
Now you accomplish, Lord, what you
    promised.
Never have you broken the promise which
you made to me.
Your grace sets us free and saves us, and
your anger punishes and drives
    away our enemies.
Faithful Lord, your faithless servant knows
this well: for all time you are just.
…
Beyond the veil of death, let me see my
people make ready for the greatest
    of feasts.
When I dive deep into your eternity,
O Lord, may I see my people marching
    towards freedom."

                            (Henkys 227f)

////////////////

*I*t was in September 1944 that Bonhoeffer
wrote this long poem (90 verses, each of
two lines — as if it was designed to be read out
antiphonally, like a liturgical psalm), of which

only a few extracts are given here. He wrote the poem in secret, addressing it to his friend Eberhard Bethge — it was among the last letters received by him from Bonhoeffer — and to his fiancée Maria von Wedemeyer. Entitled "The Death of Moses," it is concerned with a matter which had been central to Bonhoeffer long before he was forced to endure the sufferings of a Nazi prison.

In 1933, Bonhoeffer had confided to one of his students his belief that, like Jesus, he would die before reaching the age of 40. Now when Bonhoeffer wrote this poem, he had less than half a year to live: the Nazis were just about to put their hands on documents which showed the links between Bonhoeffer and the circle of anti-Hitler conspirators, and Bonhoeffer had little hope of escaping alive from their clutches.

The story of the Old Testament — set freely into verse (we see in this poem strong echoes of the *Nunc dimittis* in Lk 2:29–32) — here serves as a preparation for Bonhoeffer's own impending death. He describes the journey of Moses up Mount Nebo, where God showed him the Promised Land before he died (see Dt 34).

Not for nothing did Bonhoeffer choose an Old Testament figure, Moses. In the Germany of the 1930s, Christians blinded by raw nationalism believed that they could reconcile their religious faith with Nazism, and to this end they advocated the "de-Judaizing" of the Bible. They even went so far as to apply to the Church the Aryan Clause of 7 April 1933, which barred all "non-Aryans" (according to the openly racist criteria of the Third Reich) from public office. Several dozen pastors were evicted from office by this manifestly unjust measure.

On 13 April 1933, Bonhoeffer had publicly denounced the Aryan Clause, and underlined the duty of aid which the Church owed to victims of State brutality, whether Christians or not. In August, with his friend Franz Hildebrandt he published a pamphlet describing the Aryan Clause as "heresy for the Church," and inviting students to put into practice Proverbs 31:8: "Speak out for those who cannot speak" (see DBW 13. 204).

However, after the Nuremberg Laws of 1935, which stripped Jews of all legal rights, the Synod of the Confessing Church was reluctant to engage in open protest against the Nazi Government. According to Eberhard Bethge, it was this situation which provoked Bonhoeffer into making his famous warning, "Only those who cry out in defense of the Jews have the right to sing their Gregorian chant." During the first major deportations of Jews from Berlin, in 1941, Bonhoeffer contributed to the writing of reports aimed at keeping generals hostile to

Hitler informed, and at urging them to depose him. At the same time, Bonhoeffer was engaged in spiriting Jews away to Switzerland, and thus allowing them to escape certain death.

The poem "The Death of Moses" is not only pertinent to Bonhoeffer's story in virtue of his acts in favor of the Jews. It is also embedded in Bonhoeffer's practice of daily prayer and worship (see Day 3 and Day 5). In the Church of Prussia, in which Bonhoeffer was brought up, liturgical use of the psalter had died out long before; Bonhoeffer had compelled his young theological students at Finkenwalde Seminary to pray the psalter, morning and evening, singing the verses alternately (see DBW 5. 38 and 5. 115).

One of the themes of this poem is that God keeps his word, whether this is a word of grace or a word of judgment. God does not fail in his promises, but keeps them (see verses 10 and 79). Moses, "the man of God (see Ps 90:1) and prophet," instrument and friend of God (verse 40), asks his Creator to deliver his punishment and to give him the "long sleep of death" (verse 82). But what had Bonhoeffer done to deserve such a punishment? Had Bonhoeffer, like Moses, professed words of discouragement or impatience (verses 27–28)? According to the poem, he had not had enough trust in God.

Whatever the extent of Bonhoeffer's blame, Moses' was surely slight, in the face of the "murmurs" uttered by the people against the

"stiff-necked" one. And whatever the errors
of Bonhoeffer, broken by months of captivity
and interrogation, surely they are minor when
compared to the compromise and cowardice
of the great majority of his people, not least
those of his own church. This all seems true,
but Bonhoeffer refuses to exempt himself from
the blame attached to his people and church. In
1940, to fill the gap occupied by his own silent
church, Bonhoeffer proclaimed a Declaration
of Repentance:

> The Church confesses having witnessed
> the arbitrary use of brutal violence, the
> physical and mental suffering of innu-
> merable innocent people, oppression,
> hatred and murder, without raising its
> voice, and without making any move
> to find the means to come to anyone's
> aid. The Church has become guilty of
> the lives of the weakest of the brothers
> and sisters of Jesus Christ, and of those
> least capable of defending themselves.
> (DBW 6. 129f)

In this way, Bonhoeffer did not shy from loving his own people and from carrying their bur-
den and blame (verses 88-89). When he prayed,
he asked God to make his people into a praying
people (verse 64). A tone of hope dominates the
poem: beyond death, Moses and Bonhoeffer
can already see the advent of a new age (verse

43), which announces the grace of God over a free land (verse 53): a guilty people is called to healing, thanks to the holiness of God.

Like Moses, who led Israel out of Egypt but who did not enter the Promised Land, Bonhoeffer sees — but only from afar — the fruition of God's will to save (verse 44): a salvation born of justice, which protects the weak from random fate and from violence (verse 54) and where God's truth gathers together a scattered people (verse 55).

In his references to the Promised Land while all his personal hope seems in vain, Bonhoeffer expresses a hope for the German Church and people once the war is over. During the time that he wrote this poem, his country's future, as well as the church's, preoccupied him deeply, in a world where "the time when we can say this to humanity (i.e.: that Christ is for us) in words of theology or piety is gone forever" (DBW 8. 402: letter dated 30 April 1944 to Eberhard Bethge). The failed attempt on Hitler's life meant that Bonhoeffer's mission had not succeeded, and — like Moses — he was obliged to occupy a back seat after this. But he knew that the God of justice and grace would have the last word, and these verses look forward to this future joy.

Reflection Questions

Why was Bonhoeffer so hostile to the Nazis' Aryan Clause? Bonhoeffer saw the silence of his fellow-Christians in the face of Nazi persecution of the Jews as cowardly and hypocritical. How did he voice his criticism? How is Bonhoeffer's Declaration of Repentance of 1940 still relevant today? For Bonhoeffer, writing in 1944, what was the "Promised Land" of the German Church and people? Why, for Bonhoeffer, is the time of declaring Christ's truth in words of theology or piety gone forever? How, then, can Christ's truth now be proclaimed?

9
Morning Prayer for Fellow-Prisoners

Focus Point

///////////

Arrested on suspicion of involvement in a plot to assassinate Hitler, Bonhoeffer begins his incarceration and interrogation sustained by prayer, grateful for the small pleasures of prison life, and hoping for better times with his fiancée.

///////////

O God, early in the morning I cry to you.
Help me to pray
And to concentrate my thoughts on you;
I cannot do this alone.

In me there is darkness,
But with you there is light;
I am lonely, but you do not leave me;

I am feeble in heart, but with you there is
  help;

I am restless, but with you there is peace.
In me there is bitterness, but with you
*   there is patience;*
I do not understand your ways,
But you know the way for me.

O heavenly Father,
I praise and thank you
For rest in the night;
I praise and thank you for this new day;
I praise and thank you for all your goodness
*   and faithfulness throughout my life.*

You have granted me many blessings;
Now let me also accept what is hard
*   from your hand.*
You will lay on me no more
*   than I can bear.*
You make all things work together for good
*   for your children.*

Lord Jesus Christ,
You were poor and in distress,
*   a captive and forsaken as I am.*

You know all man's troubles;
You abide with me
*   when all men fail me;*
You remember and seek me;
It is your will that I should know you
*   and turn to you.*

Lord, I hear your call and follow;
Help me.

O Holy Spirit,
Give me faith that will protect me
    from despair, from passions, and from vice;
Give me such love for God and men
    as will blot out all hatred and bitterness;
Give me the hope that will deliver me
    from fear and faint-heartedness.

                              (DWB 8. 204–206)
                    (Bonhoeffer [English] 30–31)

///////////////

*O*n 5 April 1943, a few days after a large
family party on the occasion of the 75th
birthday of his father Karl, Dietrich Bonhoeffer
was arrested by the Gestapo. That evening, he
was incarcerated in Tegel military prison in
Berlin. What must have been his state of mind
by Christmas 1943, after eight months spent
with hundreds of prisoners, of whom twenty
or so were executed each week? The shock of
imprisonment as well as of being interrogated
under torture had nursed in him the notion of
suicide — so as not to betray his friends — before
he rejected this course of action definitively.

Even though reduced to inaction and solitude, his experience of a monastic rhythm of life
at Finkelwalde allowed him not to sink. Once

permitted to have a Bible, he read it systematically, meditating on it each day, as he had done at the seminary of the Confessing Church. He learned biblical texts by heart, as well as reciting to himself the canticles which were familiar to him. These times of meditation and of private prayer were even more important because it had been a very long time since the chapel at Tegel had seen public worship: Bonhoeffer's cell became his sole place of prayer, and he took to heart the advice given five centuries earlier by Thomas à Kempis and Gerard Groote in the *Imitation of Christ*, "Guard your cell faithfully, and it will guard you."

From 23 May 1943, Bonhoeffer benefited from regular visits from his parents (to whom he had the right to write every tenth day). In these letters, he hid from them the dark reality of Tegel: "I continue to do well.... I am well-treated, I read a lot, especially the Bible, or newspapers and novels" (DBW 8. 50: letter of 25 April 1943); "In many respects, my situation … isn't so different from what it was elsewhere: I read, I think, I work, I write, I go here and there — and all this truly without scratching the walls till I bleed, like a caged polar bear …" (DBW 8. 69: letter of 15 May 1943).

When Bonhoeffer made references to the difficulty of his situation, it was always without complaining: "… I must practice myself what I say to others in my sermons and books" (DBW 8. 55; letter of 4 May 1943). On 26 June 1943, he was even able, in sight of his jailers, to speak to his young fiancée, Maria von Wedermeyer (see Day 3 above).

As Christmas approached, Bonhoeffer remained in the uncertainty of his situation. Was he going to spend the holiday alone for the first time, far from his nearest and dearest? Was he going to taste again the freedom for which he yearned so much and which had always been present in a life of meetings and travel? Would he be allowed to begin a family with Maria, whom he had seen only on rare occasions even before his imprisonment?

We can see in Bonhoeffer's correspondence how much these thoughts must have tormented him. He had to be harsh to himself to stop his spirits sinking into despair and to help himself bear his captivity. His prayer of Christmas 1943, addressed to the trinitarian God, Father, Son and Holy Spirit, is quite remarkable in the light of this. It was at the request of the chaplain Harald Poelchau, who visited him weekly, that Bonhoeffer composed prayers for use by prisoners. The chaplains at Tegel gave them to those who requested. Written for use by others, these prayers nonetheless reveal the feelings which animated Bonhoeffer's soul.

His Morning Prayer is suffused with biblical allusions, such as the themes drawn from the Psalms of the "help," the "light," and the "ways" of God, or this verse from St. Paul's letter to the Romans, "... all things work together for the good for those who love God" (Rom 8:28). Besides, this prayer is not limited to the exclusively spiritual requests which open and close it: it is equally praise of God and gratitude to him.

God the Father, Son and Holy Spirit takes the opposite position to the prisoner's: God sheds light; he gives his presence and his help; he delivers peace and patience, since only he comprehends the prisoner's journey (see verse 2).

God the Father is praised for all things, even the things which are considered insignificant and as taken for granted in normal life, but of which in his cell the captive appreciates the full value. In this way, Bonhoeffer was granted the "repose of the night" at a time when the Allied bombings of Germany were intensifying (see verse 3).

The Son, God incarnate, had shared Bonhoeffer's wretched situation; but the Son is not just a role model or a comforting presence ("you stay there with me ..."); rather, he calls, he demands in his service even the prisoner (verse 4). It is in turning his sight towards God and towards his neighbor that he escapes self-pity.

As for the Holy Spirit, the Comforter, Bonhoeffer asks for nothing less of him than the three theological virtues of faith, hope and love. They and they only can give him the power to resist the temptations which threaten the unjustly-imprisoned prisoner: fear, despair and hatred.

Because of this, the person who prays need not ask God to break his chains or to sweep away his prison walls, but rather to free him from his inner chains, in order to discover a true and authentic freedom. This liberty, grounded in the prayer which is a confident and unselfish conversation with God, gives Bonhoeffer power to offer comfort to those near him but spared the sufferings of prison:

> If you love me, my beloved Maria, be brave — even if during Christmastide you only have this letter as proof of my love.... The message of Christmas ... tells us that what seems bad and dark is in fact good and light, because it comes from God. It is just our eyes which fool us: God is there in the manger, riches in poverty, light in darkness, help in abandonment. Nothing bad happens to us: whatever men can do to us, in all that they do they cannot help serving the God who — in ways hidden from sight — shows himself as the God of love, and who rules the universe and our lives.... My lovely Maria, let us cel-

ebrate Christmas in this spirit. When in company, be as joyful as one can only ever be at Christmas. Don't let yourself think of horrid images of me in my cell, but remember only that Christ treads through prisons — and that he will not pass by without stopping beside me.

(Brautbriefe 95;
letter of 13 December 1943)

Reflection Questions

How were Bonhoeffer's disciplines as Rector of Finkenwalde a help to him in prison? In prison, Bonhoeffer did not feel "like a caged polar bear." What enabled him to retain his sanity? How, for Bonhoeffer, is daily prayer especially relevant in prison?

10
Evening Prayer for Fellow-Prisoners

Focus Point

///////////////

As Bonhoeffer's imprisonment continues, he is thrown increasingly on God to solace his loneliness and deprivation.

///////////////

O Lord my God, thank you
for bringing this day to a close;
Thank you for giving me rest
in body and soul.
Your hand has been over me
and has guarded and preserved me.
Forgive my lack of faith
and any wrong that I have done today,
and help me to forgive all who have
*   wronged me.*

Let me sleep in peace under your protection,
and keep me from all temptations of
    darkness.

Into your hands I commend my loved ones
and all who dwell in this house;
I commend to you my body and soul.
O God, your holy name be praised.
Amen.

(DBW 8. 207)
(Bonhoeffer [English] 32)

///////////////

*I*n the loneliness of Tegel prison, Bonhoeffer maintained the disciplined prayer life which had been his practice when he enjoyed liberty. The only loneliness which troubled him was spiritual loneliness: this did make him suffer, and in a letter to Eberhard Bethge on 18 November 1943 he confided that he had been refused even the services of a chaplain (see DBW 8. 186).

All the same, Bonhoeffer assured his friend that he had not succumbed to the pitfalls to which spiritual isolation had tempted him — especially to the aridity familiar to monks — even though after the shock of imprisonment he had been isolated and treated as a criminal: the cells neighboring his own were all occupied by those condemned to death. In this spiritual resistance, the daily reading of the Bible (especially the Psalms and the Book of Revelation) and of the poetic hymns of Paul Gerhardt were a great solace to him. Bonhoeffer remained determined not to give his captors and tormentors the satisfaction of seeing him break.

To the morning call to prayer which opens the day (see Day 8), a reply comes in the evening prayer which closes it. For the night as well as for the day, Bonhoeffer places himself entirely in the hands of God. On each and every occasion, his prayer involves thanksgiving, request for forgiveness and intercession, but the emphases are placed differently. Evening prayer — briefer than morning prayer — begins with thanksgiving, whereas morning prayer begins with asking the guidance of God in order to pray.

Is it any easier to give thanks once the day is done? Doubtless yes, if like Bonhoeffer we are aware even of those gifts of the Creator which seem insignificant, aware of the most ordinary things as being the gift of God, starting with the peace of mind which God offers. Bonhoeffer did not cease to repeat this insight to his fiancée Maria: they did not have to wait for his release and their reunion (no doubt the object of their fervent prayers) in order to give thanks to God; God's gifts and his active hearing of prayer are infinitely wider than the few suggestions which we happen to make to him.

My beloved Maria, even though every day we hope and ask [God] that — soon — we'll be able to find each other and be together, don't forget even for a day to thank God for the boundless generosity of what he has given us and continues to give us each day. If you manage to do this, all our thoughts and all our projects will become clear and calm, and we will be able to bear our destiny more easily and serenely. This week's Gospel reading — on thankfulness (St. Luke 17:11–18) — is one the dearest and most important passages for me.

(Brautbriefe 64)

My dear, dear Maria, ... should we really be so impatient because many of our desires have not yet been realized, or shouldn't we rather just be happy because there are an infinity of things which allow us to grasp the goodness of God with our own hands?

(Brautebriefe 150-152)

Bonhoeffer surely remembered writing in July 1940 that "thankfulness searches beyond the gift to the giver" (DBW 16. 491). Gratitude has its origin in the love which it receives from God, before becoming "itself the source of love for God and love for people" (DBW 16. 491).

That is the reason why in Bonhoeffer's evening prayer the prayers of thanksgiving begin with confession: the "lack of faith" and the "evil deeds" of the day, which is to say the lack of love for God and for neighbor, are integral to this lack of gratitude, which renders humanity miserable.

Paraphrasing the fifth line of the Lord's Prayer, Bonhoeffer prays to God to help him to "forgive those who have wronged him." We see here a vital theme of the liturgy employed at Finkenwalde and set out in Bonhoeffer's *On Community Life*, the instruction not to let the sun go down on our anger (see Eph 4:26): every single dispute caused during the day must be resolved that evening, since "it is dangerous for a Christian to go to bed with an unreconciled heart" (DBW 5. 63). In this way, the request for forgiveness and reconciliation are essential elements in evening prayer.

The same is true for the prayer to be "preserved from the temptations of the night" found in early Christian liturgies and in the prayers included in Martin Luther's *Short Catechism* of 1529. During sleep, mankind is powerless, given up to what is dark and to the assaults of the devil. He therefore needs to ask for the help of God, or of his angels, so that, even while asleep, he may remain under the guidance of the Creator: "During our sleep also, we are either in the

hands of God or under the power of the devil"
(DBW 5. 63f).

Bonhoeffer's evening prayer did not conclude
with any selfish request, but rather in intercession for others — "I place into your care those
close to me" — and in praise — "May your holy
name be praised." We have already observed
this remarkable characteristic of Bonhoeffer's
prayers (see Day 8). Far from any self-pity, he
concerned himself with those around him:
it was they whom he worried might be more
threatened by discouragement than he, and
whom he placed under the grace and the protection of God. For himself, his prayer-requests
are less marked by any wish for improvement
in his physical lot than in the strengthening
of his faith. Whether inside or outside prison,
Bonhoeffer wished to carry on declaring to
God, "Your hand is upon me, and guards and
keeps me."

> The decision seems to have been taken:
> I cannot be with you at Christmas
> — but no one here has the courage to
> tell me. Why? Do they consider me so
> incapable of putting on a brave face? ...
> Really and truly, the question for me
> is not the more-or-less childish one of
> being or not being at my own home at
> Christmas...: I think that I would be
> able to make this sacrifice with joy if I

could make it "in faith" and if I knew that it had to be thus. ... Please do not worry in the slightest on my behalf if something even worse happens to me. It has already happened to other brothers. The real danger consists in wandering without belief, in endlessly deliberating without action, and in not wanting to dare to do anything. I need to be certain that I am in God's hands and not those of men. If this is true, everything becomes easy, even the worst deprivation.

(DBW 8. 251f: letter of
22 December 1943)

Reflection Questions

Bonhoeffer was refused the ministrations of a chaplain, and his cell was next to those of condemned prisoners awaiting execution. Why was he determined not to let his captors see him "break"? Why do you think that Bonhoeffer emphasized "thankfulness" as a spiritual response to his ongoing imprisonment? For Bonhoeffer, what made "everything ... easy, even the worst deprivation"?

11
Prayer in Time of Distress

Focus Point

////////////

Under nightly attack from Allied bombings, Bonhoeffer, through prayer rooted in the Psalms, shows a love of life, a refusal to try to manipulate God, and a steadfast concentration on the Eternal.

////////////

O Lord God,
great distress has come upon me;
and I do not know what to do.
O God, be gracious to me and help me.
Give me strength to bear what you send,
and do not let fear rule over me;
Take a father's care of those I love,
My wife and children.

O merciful God,
forgive me all the sins that I have
committed
against you and against my fellow men.
I trust in your grace
and commit my life wholly into your
hands.
Do with me according to your will
and as is best for me.
Whether I live or die, I am with you,
and you, my God, are with me.
Lord, I wait for your salvation
and for your kingdom.
Amen.

(DBW 8. 208)
(Bonhoeffer [English] 33)

////////////////

*I*n this prayer, written for fellow prisoners in a "situation of particular distress,"
Bonhoeffer relates to God in the manner of the
author of the Psalms: he immediately cries out
to his Creator and explains the situation which
is oppressing him (see for example Psalms 5, 7,
12, 55, 69 and 130). Enclosed like the Psalmist,
Bonhoeffer too, the inmate of Tegel, can see
no way out (see Psalm 88:9). Equally confined
by the walls of his cell and by his anxieties,
Bonhoeffer is overwhelmed.

Thanks to the simple and rather general
expressions Bonhoeffer uses, his fellow captives

would not have found much difficulty in apply-
ing his animated pleas to their own situation: in
the uncertainty of their future, often ignorant of
the accusations made against them, deprived of
communication among themselves, the more
aware prisoners were liable to worry every day
about the next day's outcome — would they
withstand the torture used during interroga-
tions? And, if not, didn't they risk dragging their
nearest and dearest into death? Would the Nazi
régime find evidence against them? Wouldn't it
simply invent documentary evidence? Besides,
whether they had been incarcerated in Tegel
for opposition to the régime or for less serious
reasons, all inmates lived in fear of the Allied
bombings which were beginning to strike the
capital city by night.

Their worries and fears were directed also
to their families and friends, living at liberty
but also touched by the restrictions of wartime:
"Today's attack certainly wasn't pretty. I immediately thought of you all, and in particular of
Renate. In moments like these, the gallows-
humor of prison life is pushed too far" (DBW
8. 199f), wrote Bonhoeffer to Eberhard Bethge
on 23 November 1943. On the same day, he
informed his friend of the contents of his will,
being of the opinion that it was now "reasonable
to take necessary measures" (DWB 8. 203).

On the night of 26 November 1943, a further
bombardment occurred, targeting a munitions
factory in the immediate vicinity of Tegel. In his

letters following this attack, Bonhoeffer described the panic caused by the explosions, even though they caused only injury, not death. He was amazed that afterwards the inmates spoke openly and without embarrassment of the blind fear they had felt — Bonhoeffer himself had not felt able to broach this subject except during confession, and had asked himself if this fear wasn't a shameful feeling better kept hidden (see DWB 8. 211).

On reading these lines, we understand more why Bonhoeffer asks God "not to let fear have dominion over him." He confided to Bethge on 29 November 1943 that the aerial attacks "led him back in a very basic way to prayer and to the Bible" (DBW 8. 215).

One of the characteristics of Bonhoeffer's prayer is that, once again, he does not ask God to alter his physical situation, for example, by ending the bombings, or even by bringing forward his release from prison. A few days later, without further comment, he reported the embarrassed request of a junior officer: "Minister, please pray that today there will be no air-raid sirens" (DBW 8. 227). We note that Bonhoeffer felt detatched equally from life, from freedom or from his relations with those he loved: "It is only when we love life and the world to the point that the prospect of losing them would make everything seem lost and futile, that we can believe in the resurrection of the dead and the life of the world to come" (DBW 8. 226).

Bonhoeffer did not flee from the here and now to the beyond, or — to use Bonhoeffer's own terminology — let go prematurely of current realities in favor of the last things. What was important to Bonhoeffer was that God graced him with his comforting presence. And this presence was offered in prayer itself.

For this reason, this prayer — although it opened with a cry of anguish — concludes with serene calm. By the sheer fact of having expressed to God his distress and fear, Bonhoeffer is comforted in prayer. He can now make confident requests, inspired by the intimate requests in the Lord's Prayer, "thy will be done" and "thy kingdom come" — "Do with me what you will ... Lord, I wait for your salvation and your kingdom."

Reflection Questions

Why do you think that Bonhoeffer was embarrassed to admit, after bombing raids, that he had been afraid? How does the threat of death lead us "back in a very basic way to prayer and the Bible"? Why do you think that Bonhoeffer was embarrassed by a prison officer asking him to pray that there would be no bombardments that night? When, for Bonhoeffer, does belief in the life of the world to come really become possible?

12
Who Am I?

Focus Point

////////////

As Bonhoeffer's imprisonment drags on for over a year, he is forced to confront difficult personal questions about himself — his Prussian aristocratic exterior belies a seething, despairing, humiliated inner man. Where is God in all this?

////////////

Who am I? They often tell me
I would step from my cell's confinement
calmly, cheerfully, firmly,
like a squire from his country-house.

Who am I? They often tell me
I would talk to my warders
freely and friendly and clearly,
as though it were mine to command.

Who am I? They also tell me
I would bear the days of misfortune
equably, smilingly, proudly,
like one accustomed to win.
Am I then really all that which other men
*   tell of?*
Or am I only what I know of myself,
restless and longing and sick, like a bird in
*   a cage,*
struggling for breath, as though hands were
*   compressing my throat,*
hungry for colors, for flowers, for the voices
*   of birds,*
thirsty for words of kindness, for
*   neighborliness,*
trembling with anger at despotisms and
*   petty humiliation,*
caught up in expectation of great events,
powerlessly grieving for friends at an
*   infinite distance,*
weary and empty at praying, at thinking,
*   at making,*
faint, and ready to say farewell to it all?

Who am I? This or the other?
Am I one person today, and tomorrow
*   another?*
Am I both at once? A hypocrite before
*   others,*
and before myself a contemptibly
*   woebegone weakling?*

Or is something within me still like a
  beaten army,
fleeing in disorder from victory already
  achieved?

Who am I? They mock me, these lonely
  questions of mine.
Whoever I am, thou knowest, O God,
  I am thine.

(Henkys 121f)
(Bonhoeffer [English] 130–131)

//////////////

*I*n contrast to the other poems Bonhoeffer wrote in prison, "Who am I?" refers openly to his situation as a captive: he speaks about his cell and his prison-guards; he compares himself to a caged bird. By the time he wrote this poem, imprisonment was a familiar reality for him — he had been incarcerated at Tegel for fifteen months when he wrote these words to Eberhard Bethge on 8 July 1944. In it, he puts into verse a question which had bothered him for several months:

> … I feel like I have aged several years because of what I see and hear, and the world often disgusts me and weighs me down. I often ask myself who I really am…: the man who wrings and twists himself, grinding his teeth in the middle of the horrible things which happen

here, or the man who hits himself with
a whip in order to remain — on the
outside and to his own eyes too — a
calm, serene, relaxed and aloof man,
and who, for all that — i.e.: for all this
theatrical performance, because that's
what it is — fills those around him with
admiration? In short, I know myself
less than ever. And I don't even attach
any importance to the question....

(DBW 8. 235)

So, being plunged into a strange world, of
which he simply did not know the outcome,
was leading Bonhoeffer to ask more deeply
questions about his own true identity, "Who am
I?" He begins by contrasting his practical fate
— described much more grimly than in his letter of 15 December 1943 — and the picture he
gives of a man at ease with his jailers, of a leader
accustomed to giving orders and to winning.
His attitude reminds us of one of the wealthy
landowners numbered among Bonhoeffer's
friends and acquaintances — do not forget that
Bonhoeffer himself was upper class, and was the
fiancé of Maria von Wedermeyer, whose parents were landed Prussian aristocrats. There is
no surprise in seeing this patrician tone coming
from inside Bonhoeffer's cell. More profoundly,
and independently of his social rank, Bonhoeffer
carried himself, according to the testimony of
others, with energy and calmness.

It should come as no surprise that Bonhoeffer holds such strikingly contradictory attitudes. In the Nazi prison system, which turned established social structures, whether cultural or ethical, upside-down, could Bonhoeffer truly have remained "what others say of me"? How could he have remained unaffected, after torture and under constant threat of immediate execution? To the contradiction between his wretched condition and socially-elevated bearing, Bonhoeffer adds another, deeper contradiction, between how he appeared and how he really was.

In using this language, we do not wish to make any value-judgments, nor to agree with Bonhoeffer when he calls himself "a hypocrite" in front of his neighbors. We would be wrong to see in his behavior simply a derisory attempt to save face in front of his executioners. In any case, any prisoner has to struggle to keep his dignity, and saving face — when it means resisting all that tries to break human dignity — can be a vital part of this struggle. Bonhoeffer knew this well enough:

> ... A purely external and physical discipline (morning exercises or cold baths) does help to maintain an internal discipline.... Above all, we never have the right to surrender to self-pity.
>
> *(DBW 8. 243f: letter of 18 December 1943)*

Was Bonhoeffer's attempt to keep his head high "derisory" or "hypocritical"? His own words show that when he used these terms of himself, he was being too critical.

The end of the poem shows us that it does not just serve as a prisoner's monologue but much more as a prayer. A few months earlier, in his letter to Bethge, Bonhoeffer had ended his speculations on his own identity by refusing to give a definitive answer ("There are more important things in life than to understand oneself," DBW 8. 235). But in "Who am I?" his questions lead on to an exclamation of joy, "Whoever I am, you know me: I am yours, O God!"

To reply truthfully to the question "Who am I?" involves beginning by altering the question: "Whose am I? To whom do I belong?" Because in the end those who pray recognize that God gives them their identity. Our identities are received, given. So in God, the contradiction between the personality seen by someone else and that known by the self is reconciled. Bonhoeffer's deepest identity was not changed by his months in prison; indeed, we might even claim that this miserable imprisonment allowed him to find it and to re-find it. A few days later, in a letter of 16 July 1944, among the biblical texts for sermons which Bonhoeffer suggested to Bethge, we find Psalm 119:94a, "I am yours, save me" (DBW 8. 529).

The final verses are a brief confession of faith, resembling the contents of some of the catechisms of the Reformation, which shed light on what precedes them. It is in the presence of God, right in front of God, that Bonhoeffer has asked the question about the nature of his own identity. And it is according to the light of God that such terms as the adjective *gelassen,* used in the first verses — we might translate it as "above suffering" or "relaxed" — acquire a new meaning: *Gelassenheit*, a word common in the literature of Christian mysticism, becomes much more than mere calm, and has the nuance of a trusting abandonment of self into God.

Despite being written in the context of a very specific tragedy and despite its referring to events which happened sixty years ago (we see, for example, in the lines referring to "the defeated army" a reference to the German military disaster at Stalingrad), "Who am I?" remains immensely popular today. It is still read and meditated upon in private prayer and public worship. Without being silent about his own torments in captivity, Bonhoeffer knew how to broaden questions about his own plight to encompass, in simple but moving terms, the question of the identity of all humankind — and to propose a faithful answer.

Reflection Questions

How had Bonhoeffer's "theatrical performance" of outer serenity in prison made it
harder for him truly to know himself? What
do you think that Bonhoeffer meant by saying,
"Above all, we never have the right to surrender
to self-pity"? Why did Bonhoeffer think that the
question "Whose am I?" was more useful than
"Who am I?"?

13
The Past

////////////

In prison Bonhoeffer keenly feels the absence of his fiancée, but refuses to look with nostalgia to the past: the future decided by God is his hope.

////////////

O happiness beloved, and pain beloved
   in heaviness,
you went from me.
What shall I call you? Anguish, life,
   blessedness,
part of myself, my heart — [my] past?
The door was slammed;
I hear your steps depart and slowly die
   away.
What now remains for me — torment,
   delight, desire?
This only do I know: that with you, all
   has gone.
...

Close to you I waken in the dead of night,
and start with fear —
are you lost to me once more? Is it
*   always vainly that I seek you,*
you, my past?
I stretch my hands out,
and I pray —
and a new thing now I hear:
"The past will come to you once more,
and be your life's most living part,
through thanks and repentance.
Feel in the past God's forgiveness and
*   goodness,*
pray him to keep you today and
*   tomorrow."*

(Henkys 93–96)
(Bonhoeffer [English] 114–116)

///////////

Written to Eberhard Bethge on 5 June 1944, this is the first poem Bonhoeffer wrote in prison. At the same time as sending these lines to his friend, while waiting anxiously for a verdict on his future, Bonhoeffer sent them also to Maria von Wedemeyer, his fiancée. Bonhoeffer had resigned himself to bachelorhood on account of the dangerous life he led in the service of the German resistance, but he fell in love with this young woman in 1942, when she was only eighteen years old.

Because of the age gap between Dietrich and Maria, her mother imposed on them both a probationary period of one year, during which they were not permitted to see each other. So it was that Maria gave her "yes" to Dietrich by letter, on 13 January 1943, a date which they regarded as their engagement.

Because he had faithfully observed the condition laid down by Ruth von Wedermeyer, Dietrich was unable to see Maria before his arrest on 5 April 1943. After this time, their next meeting took place in the prison visiting room at Tegel on 24 June 1943. Until 23 August 1944, Maria and Dietrich were granted eighteen brief encounters, always in the presence of a guard. That said, they conducted an active correspondence, marked by great tenderness and depth of feeling. This correspondence was published only in 1992, and is a remarkable collection of letters which throws new light on Bonhoeffer's last years.

Written in between two of these meetings, "The Past" is nonetheless much more than a nostalgic reverie on the happy and brief times when the two young people could speak freely in the house belonging to Maria's grandmother. Although Maria features throughout the poem, it cannot be seen as Dietrich's paean of praise to his fiancée. Maria is not identified with the past (in German, the word *Vergangenheit* is feminine), even if certain terms in the poem might suggest it: "… I hear steps walking further away and slowly being lost to silence. What is left for me? Joy? Torment? Desire? I only know one thing: you went away, and all is past" (Henkys 93). From this long poem, we have reproduced just the beginning, which gives the general tenor, and the closing lines, which (as Dietrich explained to Maria) were the most important and which were the origin of the entire poem.

The theme of the past is not Bonhoeffer's own. In the prison writings of political detainees, the past generally occupies a pivotal place: to hang onto their memories helps them to withstand the extreme conditions of confinement; to immerse themselves in the world of the past allows them not to lose their equilibrium entirely. In his letters to Maria, Bonhoeffer insists on the fact that we must not lose our sense of the past: it belongs to us and must remain part of us — the past is *our* past. It abides thanks to our acknowledgement that it is God who gives all good gifts, and thanks to our sorrow for the ways in which we spoil those gifts.

Bonhoeffer writes, "We must unceasingly purify the past completely by washing it in thanks and contrition" (*Brautbriefe* 176). It is by means of this that we can think over the past without remorse and even draw strength from our memories. In his first letter to Eberhard

Bethge, on 18 November 1943, Bonhoeffer spoke of the need to make one's past present, in a situation where time appeared empty and lost to him. Already in this letter, he called for both thanksgiving and repentance (see DBW 8. 188f).

In the light of these considerations, the first lines of the poem, apparently surprising, take on all their true sense. For a prisoner placed daily in fear of his life (although see Day 12 for another view of this), to complain that he does not have a future is natural. But how then do we explain that he regrets the loss of his past? In the letter he wrote to Bethge on 5 June 1944, Bonhoeffer expresses the fear of this loss, especially during the long periods which separated one prison-visit from another; wrestling with the past and trying to hold onto it, and even to recreate it, constituted Bonhoeffer's daily life in prison (DBW 8. 466f).

As the rest of the poem shows, it was in prison that Bonhoeffer was able to see the whole value of his past. He did not do this in a cloud of nostalgia, but with simple gratitude. To remind oneself of one's past does not negate the suffering of the present moment, but it does fill in its emptiness. Whereas Maria quite understandably regretted that her moments of happiness with Dietrich were all too fleeting and belonged to the past, Bonhoeffer himself stressed the gratitude which those moments ought to engender. This is a gratitude which lasts into the present, triggered by the loving presence of God.

In a letter written on 29 and 30 May 1944, a few days before this poem was posted, Bonhoeffer had given full flow to his thanksgiving: he thanked Maria for all that she had given him the previous few days, for her letter and for her presence (during her visit, they had talked about the past calmly), and more fundamentally for her love. All that he had written, he went on, should be seen as none other than thanks to Maria; he had been lucky enough to be allowed to love and to be loved, to be content in this love and to hope for its fulfillment (see *Brautbriefe* 189–191).

In the prayer which closes this poem (although the whole work should be seen as a prayer), Bonhoeffer offers gestures — "I hold out my hands" — and words: thanksgiving, acknowledgement, request for forgiveness, repentance. But why does he address these thoughts to a single other person? Why does he refer to God only obliquely, in the third person? Why, in the middle of a prayer, does he include this final exhortation to pray?

Perhaps here the dialogue between Bonhoeffer and God is opened to others. Perhaps Bonhoeffer is inviting his readers — beginning with Maria and Eberhard — to find in turn, in their own past, all that God now offers them. He equally directs them to ask for God's protection, an intercession he himself made each day in evening prayer (see Day 10). The theme of protection will return in an even more obvious way in another of Bonhoeffer's prayer-poems, "The Forces of Goodness (*Von guten Mächten*)."

When he considers his own past, Bonhoeffer is not self-absorbed: he is focused on God and on those he loves. He is assured of the reality of God's presence which — despite appearances — does not belong to a past now dead, but is active here and now and opens the way to a real hope for the future.

Reflection Questions

Why are we tempted to concentrate on the past and to live through reverie? In what sense does Bonhoeffer have to wrestle with his past in prison, as well as try to recreate it? In prison, unable to see his fiancée alone and facing the possibility of a mock-trial and execution, how was Bonhoeffer's approach to Maria von Wedermeyer one of thanksgiving?

14
The Forces of Goodness (1)

Focus Point

////////////

As Bonhoeffer faces his second Christmas in prison, he writes a poem to make his family present to him.

////////////

With every power for good to stay and
  guide me,
comforted and inspired beyond all fear,
I'll live these days with you in thought
  beside me,
and pass, with you, into the coming year.

The old year still torments our hearts,
  unhastening;
the long days of our sorrow still endure;
Father, grant to the souls thou hast
  been chastening

that thou hast promised, the healing
*   and the cure.*

Should it be ours to drain the cup of
*   grieving*
even to the dregs of pain, at thy command,
we will not falter, thankfully receiving
all that is given by thy loving hand.

(Henkys 262)
(Bonhoeffer [English] 151)

//////////////

*O*n 19 December 1944, Bonhoeffer finished his last letter to Maria with a poem. "Here are a few lines which came to me over the last few evenings. It's the message of Christmas for you and for your parents and brothers and sisters" (*Brautbriefe* 209). Make no mistake: the writing of these "few lines," informed by Bonhoeffer's grounding in the Bible, in Lutheran hymn-writing (as in the hymn of Gottfried Arnold, *So führst du doch recht selig, Herr, die deinen*) and in general literature, had been a long time in composition. Bonhoeffer had been transferred on 8 October 1944 to the prison of the Gestapo headquarters, in Berlin, and had to endure a much harsher prison régime (contrary to what he wrote to Maria). He used this astonishingly serene poem to make himself present to his family at Christmas, and to lay before them everything he owed them. Even though for the second year in succession he missed his family and friends terribly, his poem had the aim of expressing powerfully how much "he felt the links which bound [him] to [them]" (*Brautbriefe* 208) and how much these links brought him peace, comfort and happiness.

In his letter to Maria, Bonhoeffer insists on the fact that he had never felt himself alone and abandoned: his fiancée, his parents, his friends and his students were always present, through their prayers and their thoughts, just as they had been present physically in earlier conversations. Here we see again the theme of the vital importance of the past in order not to sink into the difficulties of the present. Bonhoeffer speaks of a "great, invisible Kingdom ... whose reality is undoubted" (*Brautbriefe* 208).

The words of the first verse, "surrounded ... by the forces of goodness," take up the theme of the letter, that adults as much as children are protected night and day by "benevolent and invisible powers" (*Brautbriefe* 208). We are to understand that these benevolent, protective powers are all dear and close beings who, although far from Bonhoeffer, care about him. Whether "spirits," "powers," or "angels," they are — as shown in verse 7 (see Day 15) — the instruments used by God to protect his own. In thinking of his nearest and dearest, Bonhoeffer no doubt remembers the promises of the Psalter, "You hem me in, behind and before, and lay your hand upon me" (Ps 139:5) and "He will command his angels concerning you to guard you in all your ways" (Ps 91:11).

That said, the joy experienced by the captive is not a running-away from the world, as the second verse shows, where Bonhoeffer has a prayerful dialogue with God. Suffering and evil are not hidden; rather, it is in the context of suffering and evil that prayer for salvation takes its full meaning. Bonhoeffer also avoids putting too great a stress on his own torments, not only because his correspondence was subject to a Nazi censor, but also and above all to reassure his family and friends by showing them that they and he shared the same practical situation. For them and for him, the sheer weight of the difficult days was a test of faith in the "forces of goodness" — but they like he were promised the salvation prepared by God.

Verse 3, with its plaintive "And if…," reminds us that this salvation should not be confused with simple happiness. The allusion to the bitter cup which Jesus had to drink is a reminder that all Christians have a calling to cling "close to God in his Passion" (see Day 7). This "cup of suffering" is not reserved for Bonhoeffer: it is surely Maria's too, to whom Bonhoeffer had written just a little earlier, "It is now almost two years that we have waited for each other, my beloved Maria. Do not lose heart!" (*Brautbriefe* 209).

But for Bonhoeffer, to the extent that everything which befalls them comes from "good, good hands" (*Brautbriefe* 202: letter of 13 August 1944), God will give them the promised salvation, even in the worst of cases. Following the example of Jesus at Gethsemane, Bonhoeffer does not resist the tragic outcome of the granting of some prayers.

Reflection Questions

Once transferred to the Gestapo prison, Bonhoeffer realized that his hopes of survival were slim. How has he managed to write such a serene poem as this? What allusions are there in this poem to the experience of Christ in Gethsemane? Do we see in this poem an acceptance by Bonhoeffer of his own imminent death?

15
The Forces of Goodness (2)

Focus Point

////////////

At his final Christmas, Bonhoeffer celebrates his communion with all God's children, and steels himself to face martyrdom.

////////////

But should it be thy will once more to release us
to life's enjoyment and its good sunshine,
that which we've learned from sorrow shall increase us,
and all our life be dedicated as thine.

Today let candles shed their radiant greeting;
lo, on our darkness are they not thy light

leading us, haply, to our longed-for meeting?

Thou canst illumine even our darkest night.

When now the silence deepens for our
    hearkening,
grant we may hear thy children's voices
    raise
from all the unseen world around us
    darkening
their universal paean, in thy praise.

While all the powers of good aid and
    attend us,
boldly we'll face the future, come what may.
At even and at morn God will befriend us,
and oh, most surely on each newborn day!

(Henkys 263)
(Bonhoeffer [English] 151)

///////////////

*B*onhoeffer hoped and prayed that he would be allowed to see those he loved one more time, even for a few moments in the prison meeting-room. Even though he had submitted himself to the will of God, and was willing to drink from the cup of martyrdom, he did not grasp martyrdom unthinkingly. These verses express one of Bonhoeffer's fundamental beliefs: however ardent the desire for eternal fulfillment and for the salvation promised by God, the present moment, the moment of "this world and its daybreak," remains supreme.

But gratitude for God applies as much for his unseen gifts, beginning with the presence in life of "the forces of goodness," as for the visible fruits of his loving creation. Hope for the life to come does not strip our present life of value, whatever its pains. The past which Bonhoeffer wants to remember is not unlimited joy; quite the contrary. But whether it is in misfortune or in happiness, in loneliness or in company, in the present or in the future, Bonhoeffer commits his life to God: "And commit all our future to you."

Verses 5 and 6 are suffused with the calm, limpid and warm atmosphere of Christmas. Bonhoeffer is happy to depict the candles and the sounds of Christmas, beginning with the carols sung in church or at home on Christmas Eve. Christmas is the time of year where the hope to be surrounded by family and friends is at its strongest; and this implies a sadness not only for Dietrich, far from his own in the cell on the Prinz-Albrecht-Strasse, but also for Maria, whose father and mother had died on the Russian front, and also for Bonhoeffer's parents, whose son and son-in-law were incarcerated by the Gestapo.

Christmas Night could equally trigger regret and bitterness, as it underlines the unbearable contradiction of the ideal of the joyful family united around the Christmas tree in song and prayer, and the grim reality of a home missing the dead and the imprisoned, victims all of the brutality of the Nazi régime. Bonhoeffer resolves

this contradiction in the silence which sees new
voices raised even as the Christmas carols die
down and the candles are snuffed out. This is
less an allusion to the choirs of angels heard by
joyful shepherds on the first Christmas morning
(see Lk 2:13–14) than to the "voice of the world":
the voice of the disappeared, the voice of loved
ones, but also the voice of the young theological
students and ministers of the Confessing Church,
brought to life by the war unleashed by Hitler.
Right now, God nullifies the separations which
make his children suffer; Christmas is no longer
a time of tearing-apart and regret, but already
the time of a great communion. Those fortunate
enough to celebrate Christmas with their nearest
and dearest are no longer separated from the rest
of God's children.

In the same way, Bonhoeffer lets those dear
to him know that he is not alone. He also par-
takes in this vast unseen communion (see verse
7). At the end of his poem, Bonhoeffer leaves
his dialogue with God and embarks on a deep
confession of faith. He feels the assurance of
being "protected" by the forces of goodness;
the term *geborgen* conveys the sense of security
felt by a child in the family home. Deprived of
this security of home and hearth at Christmas
1944, Bonhoeffer claims a higher protection:
that of the "forces of goodness" which in the
final analysis allude to divine guidance. This
paradoxical assurance lends to the captive who

awaits summary execution the ability to face the future with serenity.

Written by Bonhoeffer with a view to comforting those near to him, these seven verses, which lack a title, have become under their assumed title of "Von guten Mächten / the Forces of Goodness," "the spiritual poem of the Twentieth-century" (see Henkys 263). Set to music — to at least fifty melodies — they have been incorporated into the church's liturgy, as well as being printed in the press as part of the Notices of Deaths. From 1959, the official German Lutheran hymn-book has included these words. Written in a place of fear and hopelessness, this intimate, simple and deep text has become, for a generation of Christians, a personal prayer of peace, comfort and hope in the face of suffering, grief and death.

Reflection Questions

What was cheerful for Bonhoeffer at his final Christmas? Which Christmas voices did Bonhoeffer most highly prize? Why do you think that this poem has become such a treasured part of modern German Lutheran liturgy? What sort of man was Dietrich Bonhoeffer?

Bonhoeffer,
Witness of Grace
and Disciple of Christ

Since July 1998, a statue of Dietrich Bonhoeffer, Bible open in his outstretched hand, has been placed above the Great West Door of Westminster Abbey. The Anglican Church honors this Protestant theologian as one of the major martyrs of the Twentieth-century. All the same, we must guard against putting Bonhoeffer on a pedestal by making him just a brave and untouchable hero. Certainly, his brief life bears witness to courageous acts and to an impressive foresight about the implications of Nazism; but also to hesitations — even perhaps to a lack of courage — as his flight to England in 1933 and to America in 1939 indicate.

Bonhoeffer, who always viewed himself without flattery, wrote at the end of 1942, "We have been the dumb witnesses of evil acts." Even if he raised his voice against Nazi ideology with more force than shown by others, he counted himself among those "dumb witnesses" who had not done enough. His prayer is therefore even more precious to us because it does not spare its own doubts, suffering and anguish.

Bonhoeffer is close to us especially when he borrows the sorrowful tones of the prophet Jeremiah: his words underline the fact that the believer is not the master of his own fate, but someone for whom God has won a victory. Bonhoeffer is a model of faith through his self-abandonment to God, as well as through the common purpose of his acts and his thought. Unusually for a theologian, he did not just write a good book about walking the way of Christ; he put into practice his faith in the unconditional obedience demanded by the Son of God, to the extent that, without actively courting martyrdom, he took responsibility for the lethal consequences of his Christian discipleship.

The incomplete status of Bonhoeffer's thought also places us in front of the demands of God, without escaping his "tough grace." In the footsteps of Christ, the prayers of Bonhoeffer and his life — or better, his life of prayer — pose the question of relief from suffering sharply: "My Father, if it is possible, let this cup pass from me; yet not what I want but what you want" (Mt 26:39). Bonhoeffer never ceased drawing a distinction between human desires and the will of God. But need they be necessarily opposed?

This harrowing question has tormented every Christian whose prayers remain unanswered. Cannot the God of all creation intervene in the world to change the course of events? Does he content himself with giving those who pray the necessary force to discern his presence in raw facts which seem to deny it, and with supporting them in adversity? Isn't the God who dies on the Cross also the God who frees his people from slavery in Egypt, and who in Jesus Christ heals the sick, raises Lazarus from the dead, and frees St. Peter from prison?

Advocate of a "faith come of age," Bonhoeffer proclaimed that the supreme answer to prayer consists in communion with God. This does not mean that Bonhoeffer was removed from the world: he gave thanks for the gifts of God here below, beginning with the "forces of goodness," his loved ones and friends. Rooted in God, Bonhoeffer was open to the "godless" who thought that they could abandon the "hypothesis of God": far from despising their hopes or from abdicating his responsibility to bear witness to the grace of God, Bonhoeffer was a martyr in terms and acts comprehensible to non-believers.

This presence for others, this "service on behalf of the world," was anchored in a life measured by regular common prayer. Even in the total solitude of the Tegel prison, Bonhoeffer preserved this spiritual discipline. By rediscovering the liturgical riches of the Fathers, he offered to other Christians refreshed vertical and horizontal axes for the Church: conceding nothing to the siren voices of individualism and of immediacy, these axes were constructed across space and across time. Far from fixing communication with God in sterile formulae, Bonhoeffer's common prayer demonstrated the extent of his horizon — the eternal banquet of the end of time in the Kingdom of God.

Bibliography

Bonhoeffer's Complete Works

The complete works of Dietrich Bonhoeffer, *Dietrich Bonhoeffer Werke,* have been published in 16 volumes (1986–1996) by Christian Kaiser (Munich).

Other editions of Bonhoeffer's Works

Brautbriefe Zelle 92. Dietrich Bonhoeffer, Maria von Wedemeyer, 1943-1945. Edited by Ruth Alice von Bismarck and Ulrich Kabitz, Munich: Beck, 1992.

Bonhoeffer Brevier. Edited by Otto Dudzus, Munich, Kaiser, 1991 (7th edition).

Some English Translations of Bonhoeffer's Works

Bonhoeffer, Dietrich. *Ethics.* London, SCM Press, 1963.

____. *Letters and Papers from Prison* (Enlarged edition). London, SCM Press, 1971. (Abridged edition), London, SCM Press, 2001.

____. *Discipleship.* Minneapolis, Fortress Press, 2004.

____. *Life Together/Prayerbook of the Bible.* Minneapolis, Fortress Press, 1996.

Studies on Bonhoeffer

Ackermann, Josef. *Dietrich Bonhoeffer — Freiheit hat offene Augen. Eine Biographie*. Gütersloher Verlagshaus, Gütersloh, 2005.

Arnold, Matthieu, ed.. *Chrétiens et Églises face au nazisme: entre adhésion et résistance*. Strasbourg, Faculté de Théologie protestante, 2005.

Bethge, Eberhard. Dietrich Bonhoeffer. *Theologe — Christ — Zeitgenosse. Eine Biographie*. Gütersloh, Gütersloher Verlagshaus, 2005 (9th edition). English translation: Dietrich Bonhoeffer: *A Biography*. Philadelphia, Fortress Press, 2000.

Burtness, James H. *Shaping the Future: Ethics of Dietrich Bonhoeffer*. Philadephia: Fortress Press, 1985.

Doering-Manteuffel, Anselm and Joachim Mehlhausen, eds. *Christliches Ethos und der Widerstand gegen den Nationalsozialismus in Europa*. Stuttgart: Kohlhammer, 1995.

Dramm, Sabine. *V-Mann Gottes und der Abwehr? Dietrich Bonhoeffer und der Widerstand*. Gütersloh: Gütersloher Verlagshaus, 2005.

Dumas, André. *Une théologie de la réalité: Dietrich Bonhoeffer. Genève: Labor et Fides*, 1968. English translation: André Dumas, *Dietrich Bonhoeffer: Theologian of Reality*. London: SCM Press, 1971.

Grin, Edmond. *"Une morale pas comme les autres: introduction à l'Éthique de Bonhoeffer." Études théologiques et religieuses* 40 (1965): 192–208 and 255–276.

de Gruchy, John W. *The Cambridge Companion to Dietrich Bonhoeffer*. Cambridge University Press, 1999.

Haynes, Stephen R. *The Bonhoeffer Phenomenon: Portraits of a Protestant Saint*. London: SCM Press, 2004.

Henkys, Jürgen. *Geheimnis der Freiheit. Die Gedichte Dietrich Bonhoeffers aus der Haft. Biographie — Poesie — Theologie*. Gütersloh: Gütersloher Verlagshaus, 2005.

Kelly, Geffrey B. *Liberating Faith, Bonhoeffer's Message for Today*. Minneapolis: Augsburg, 1984.

Merlio, Gilbert. *Les résistances allemandes à Hitler*. Paris: Tallandier, 2001.

Mottu, Henry. *Dietrich Bonhoeffer*. Paris: Cerf, 2002.

Plant, Stephan. *Bonhoeffer*. London and New York: Continuum, 2004.

Rasmussen, Larry. *Dietrich Bonhoeffer: His Significance for North Americans*. Minneapolis: Fortress Press, 1990.

Schlingensiepen, Ferdinand. *Dietrich Bonhoeffer 1906-1945. Une biographie*. Paris: Salvator, 2005.

Schmädeke, Jürgen and Peter Steinbach, eds. *Der Widerstand gegen den Nationalsozialismus. Die deutsche Gesellschaft und der Widerstand gegen Hitler*. Munich: Piper, 1994 (3rd ed.; 1st ed., 1985).

Scholder,Klaus. *Die Kirchen und das Dritte Reich*. Frankfurt: Ullstein, 1977.

Stegemann, Wolfgang, ed. *Kirche und Nationalsozialismus* (2nd revised ed.). Stuttgart, Berlin and Cologne: W. Kohlhammer, 1992 (1991).

Ueberschär, Gerd, ed. *Der deutsche Widerstand gegen Hitler. Wahrnehmung und Wertung in Europa und in den USA*. Darmstadt: Wissenschaftliche Buchgesellschaft, 2002.

Wind, Renate. *Dietrich Bonhoeffer: A Spoke in the Wheel*. Grand Rapids: Eerdmans, 1992.

Also available in the
"15 Days of Prayer" series:

Saint Augustine *(Jaime García)*
0-7648-0655-6, paper

Saint Benedict *(André Gozier)*
978-1-56548-304-0, paper

Saint Bernadette of Lourdes *(François Vayne)*
978-1-56548-314-9, paper

Saint Bernard *(Emery Pierre-Yves)*
978-0764-805745, paper

Saint Catherine of Siena *(Chantal van der
   Plancke and Andrè Knockaert)*
978-156548-310-1, paper

Pierre Teilhard de Chardin *(André Dupleix)*
978-0764-804908, paper

The Curé of Ars *(Pierre Blanc)*
978-0764-807138, paper

Saint Dominic *(Alain Quilici)*
978-0764-807169, paper

Saint Katharine Drexel *(Leo Luke Marcello)*
978-0764-809231, paper

Don Bosco *(Robert Schiele)*
978-0764-807121, paper

Charles de Foucauld *(Michael Lafon)*
978-0764-804892, paper

Saint Francis de Sales *(Claude Morel)*
978-0764-805752, paper

Saint John of the Cross *(Constant Tonnelier)*
978-0764-806544, paper

Saint Faustina Kowalska *(John J. Cleary)*
978-0764-807916, paper

Saint Louis de Montfort *(Veronica Pinardon)*
978-0764-807152, paper

Saint Martín de Porres: A Saint of the Americas *(Brian J. Pierce)*
978-0764-812163, paper

Meister Eckhart *(André Gozier)*
978-0764-806520, paper

Thomas Merton *(André Gozier)*
978-0764-804915, paper

Saint Elizabeth Ann Seton *(Betty Ann McNeil)*
978-0764-808418, paper

Johannes Tauler *(André Pinet)*
978-0764-806537, paper

Saint Teresa of Ávila *(Jean Abiven)*
978-0764-805738, paper

Saint Thérèse of Lisieux *(Constant Tonnelier)*
978-0764-804922, paper

Saint Thomas Aquinas *(André Pinet)*
978-0764-806568, paper